GW01086506

WALKING IN AN
SLOUGh

By Stuart Montgomery

CONTENTS

INTRODUCTION

This book describes a series of themed walks in and around the town of Slough, in south-east England.

It is a revised and updated version of an e-book that was published through Amazon Kindle in April 2013 with the title *Ten Top Walks in and Around Slough*. That title was intended to convey the often jokey style in which the e-book was written, by jokily deploying a naff internetty sort of tag. But it was a bad choice, for it soon became obvious that potential readers simply thought that *Ten Top Walks* would be a naff sort of book, and as a result they didn't buy it.

For this new, and retitled, version I have taken the opportunity to add some fresh words and to correct and improve some of the old text. And I have re-drawn all the maps, now employing Adobe Illustrator rather than the OCAD package that was used before.

But I have not changed the rules that guided the original version. These are:
- routes should be themed around aspects of local history or culture.
- all routes should be based on public-access footpaths.
- road-walking should be kept to a minimum.
- all walks should be accessible by public transport.
- it should be possible to shorten any walk.
- the selection of walks should include most parts of the Borough.
- all walks should start or finish within the Borough but need not be in the Borough for all their length.
- catchment boundaries are: to the north the M40, to the east the M25, to the south and west the River Thames. (On one occasion, at the start of the *Way of the Puppets*, I have broken this rule.)
- route descriptions can generally assume that the reader knows the area well enough to get to the starting point.
- heritage is vitally important as a concept, but it should be eclectic and unstuffy. ABC walks (Another Bloody Church) should be avoided at all cost.

The last point, about *heritage*, is fundamental. In many walkers' guidebooks there can be a tendency to focus disproportionately on apparently venerable stuff like castles, churches and old (or even *olde*) pubs. But I don't believe we need to limit ourselves like that, and I don't believe we should.

In the case of Slough, heritage can justifiably include puppet TV shows, grimy waterways, brick-making yards, eccentric pagan people, posh schools, prostitutes and punk rock writers.

Of course, a balanced view of the Borough's heritage should have room for the castles and churches and old pubs as well. But I believe that it is important to be open-minded and questioning about such things, rather than simply to accept them at their own valuation, which may be biased and flawed — and very often is.

* * *

In spite of the town's generally unromantic reputation, good walking routes do exist in and around Slough and some of them are surprisingly attractive. And there is a surprisingly large number of footpaths. I have known many of them for a long time — from leisure walking and also from a period in which I led groups of Nordic walkers and taught navigation courses.

Other footpaths were new to me when I started work on this guidebook. But in the course of preparing it I walked every route several times, to confirm that the itinerary was worthwhile, to try detours and alternatives, and to record and check the description. (Much web-searching was done too, and I also used to the full the excellent local studies section of Slough Library.)

I want to acknowledge that many of "my" routes have appeared, at least in part, in other walking guides. I'm not claiming to have discovered anything new. All I have tried to do is put together existing routes in new ways.

The descriptions and sketch maps should be enough to get you round, but you should also use the local Ordnance Survey maps, at a scale of 1:25,000. Unfortunately our area is covered by two OS sheets and many routes extend inconveniently between them. Rather than buying both, it makes sense to order a single bespoke sheet. For more details, go to the Ordnance Survey's website and find the entry for "custom made maps".

Kit and Clothing

Later we'll learn that the philosopher Thoreau warns us to "avoid any enterprise that requires a new set of clothes." In general that's sound advice for the occasional walker. Most of us will already have good enough clothing and footwear, at least for short walks in summer weather.

However in wintry conditions you will need boots and good quality foul-weather gear. In all seasons a compass is handy, as well as knowledge of how to use it. At the very least, it is important to know whether you are going east or west, north or south.

Personal Safety

Many people are fearful about walking in and around Slough and I'm often asked about safety. In my own experience the biggest threat comes not from hooligans or muggers but from cyclists and motorists. While researching this book I was hit by a bike and had several near misses with cars. But no-one tried to rob or assault me.

Nevertheless it is wise to take precautions. Being constantly alert to possible threats is sensible, as is having a vividly clear picture of how you would respond to them. Not going alone is also sensible (although I usually do). Leaving items like credit cards and wallets at home is prudent.

Some of the routes involve road-crossings. I have not felt the need to advise you to *carefully* cross each road, as has become the idiom in modern guidebooks. I prefer to believe that your own common sense will remind you that care is always needed. Occasionally I have added a warning, if a crossing-point seems especially perilous.

Timings

In the route descriptions the timings do not include rest stops and they generally assume an average walking speed of four kilometres per hour. (I've worked in metric because the OS maps are metric.) You should treat these times as a guide, not as a target.

* * *

While I hope that regular walkers will find new and interesting ideas in these pages, I'm also writing for people who have never tucked trouser into sock or thermos into backpack. I'd like to coax them out on to the footpaths. Partly this is for reasons of the virtue-is-its-own-reward sort. Walking does us good, after all, and so does learning about our surroundings. But it also reflects a concern that our environment is under pressure, and a belief that we will safeguard it better by more frequently connecting with it.

Stuart Montgomery

Slough, October 2015

ABOUT THE AUTHOR

After many years' experience of hill-walking and mountaineering in his native Scotland, Stuart Montgomery worked as a leader of overseas walking and cross-country skiing groups for a travel company called Waymark Holidays, which was at that time based in London. When Waymark relocated to Slough in 1990 Stuart did likewise, eventually becoming Managing Director of the company.

After Waymark was taken over by a larger organisation, Stuart co-founded a new company which organised activity holidays and which continued trading until 2014. During that time he held instructor qualifications in Nordic skiing, Nordic walking and mountain navigation.

Other books written by Stuart Montgomery include:

• *Stride and Glide: A Manual of Cross-Country Skiing and Nordic Walking*, co-written with Paddy Field and published in 2006.

• *Nordic Notes*, a collection of articles on cross-country skiing and Nordic walking, published in 2013.

• *The Red Mitten*, a novel set in Norway, published in 2015.

WALK 1

The Way Of The Puppets

John Betjeman's famous poetic put-down about Slough being unfit for humans undoubtedly upset the town's hominid inhabitants. But perhaps it helped open the way for the puppets, which spread into the area from the west in the late 1950s, their progress facilitated by film-makers Gerry and Sylvia Anderson. This walk links the sites of four studios used by the Andersons, who started their marionetting career with Twizzle, Torchy and Four Feather Falls, then worked their way through Supercar, Fireball XL5, Stingray, Thunderbirds, Captain Scarlet & the Mysterons and Joe 90.

At its peak the Anderson enterprise employed around 250 people — and a whole lot of puppets — and some of the film series have attracted a cult following. Today a large club of "Fandersons" helps keep the memory alive.

The walk mostly follows paths and country lanes, but also includes some green ways through the town — as well as some that are not so green.

Distance: 14km.   *Time:* 3.5 hours.

Start point: Maidenhead Bridge, on the A4 (Bath Road).

Finish point: A4 (Bath Road) near Leigh Road.

Transport to start: No 75 bus from Slough bus station.

Transport from end: No 75 bus to Slough bus station.

Surfaces: Mainly tarmac on sections 1 and 5. In other sections a mix of tarmac paths and earth paths, the latter sometimes narrow and uneven.

Facilities on the way: On the Maidenhead section there are pubs and a café. In Taplow there is a pub. Burnham has pubs, cafes and shops. On Slough Trading Estate there is a row of shops close to the end of the walk.

Can I shorten it? You can stop at Burnham village and take a bus to Slough, or stop at Burnham station and take a train.

Any unpleasant sections? The last section, after Burnham station, is not attractive, and you will enjoy it only if you have a very keen interest in the Anderson story.

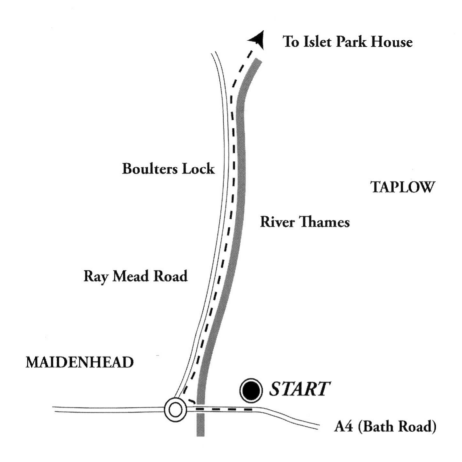

To Islet Park House

Boulters Lock

TAPLOW

River Thames

Ray Mead Road

MAIDENHEAD

START

A4 (Bath Road)

Section 1   Maidenhead Bridge to Islet Park and back

Distance: 4km roundtrip   Time: 60 minutes

Get off the bus just before Maidenhead Bridge. Without crossing the road, walk over the bridge then go immediately down steps beside Thames Riviera Hotel. Then turn through an arch in the bridge and come into a small park, called Bridge Gardens.

Go diagonally through the park and come to Ray Mead Road. Turn right, go carefully along a narrow pavement for 50m and then turn right again, into an alley that takes you back to the river.

Now turn left and follow the footway along the river bank, passing Boulters Lock and Ray Mill Island, until you come to a spot where the road veers to the left and away from the river. It will take you about 15 minutes to get here from Maidenhead Bridge.

Leave the road and turn right on an earth path along the riverside. After 10 minutes you cross a stream on a small bridge with metal railings. Here you are beside Islet Park House, a large Edwardian mansion now converted into flats.

The building's grand exterior gives no hint that it once contained a busy street in a busy town where stretchy puppet-boy Twizzle lived happily in a toy shop, until a spoiled little girl came in to buy him. Escaping under the cover of darkness, the boy befriended a stripey-footed cat and together they enjoyed many adventures.

And once all of that had settled down, Islet Park House went on to host Mr Bumbledrop's playground, whose idyllic calm was shattered when another spoiled little girl sent into Space all the kids' toys, together with the old man's straight-haired poodle. Disconsolate, the lonely Bumbledrop declared, memorably, "I know, I'll make a toy-boy", and set about creating Torchy.

These excitements happened at the command of Gerry Anderson and his partner in AP Films, Arthur Provis. In 1957 the pair had started to work on puppet films for the new medium of television. The Adventures of Twizzle and Torchy the Battery Boy were great successes and, feeling on the crest of a wave, Gerry wanted to buy Islet Park House when it came on the market in 1960. The asking price for house, furniture and 10-acre garden was only £16,500, but Arthur thought the prospect was too risky.

The disagreement contributed to the breakup of the partnership, and Gerry moved AP Films to new premises on Slough Trading Estate.

Islet Park House

If you want to see the other side of Islet Park House, retrace your steps from the little bridge for 50m and turn right, along a broad gravel track. Then go right, into Islet Park Drive then right again. Islet Park House will be in front of you.

Please respect the sign that says "Private property — do not trespass". And keep an eye out for exotic wildlife. When the film-makers decamped from Islet Park they left behind a grass snake that they had painted to resemble a rattlesnake, for their new venture, Four Feather Falls.

Now retrace your steps to Maidenhead Bridge.

Maidenhead Bridge

Section 2 Maidenhead Bridge to Taplow

Distance: 1.5km   Time: 20 minutes

Cross Maidenhead Bridge and turn immediately left along Mill Lane. In 200m, at a bend in the road, turn right on to a tarmac path. After a gas storage tank cross the Jubilee River on a foot bridge, continue uphill on the tarmac path and soon come again on to Mill Lane.

Turn right. Then at the junction with Berry Hill turn left and in two minutes reach Stockwells, a cul-de-sac.

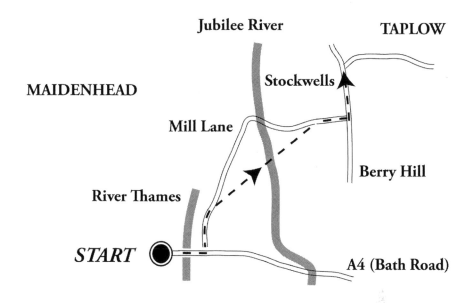

This is where, prior to the move to Islet Park, the AP Films team first came together, in a decaying old mansion that has now been demolished.

Gerry Anderson had come here in 1955 as an employee of Polytechnic Studios, mainly to work on a series of TV documentaries about eccentric Europeans. In Austria there was a man who had lived in a bottle for a year, in Germany a man who could hypnotise alligators, and somewhere else a man with no arms who played honky-tonk piano with his toes.

Surprisingly, or perhaps not, the project was not a success and Gerry and his Polytechnic colleague Arthur Provis then started a new company, Pentagon Films, still working out of Stockwells.

It was after Pentagon in turn went bust that the pair set up AP Films and moved to Islet Park (together with Sylvia Thamm, their secretary and Gerry's future wife).

In his biography Gerry Anderson said that the Stockwells property was riddled with dry-rot: climbing the stairs your foot could go through the woodwork. Alas, no trace of the old mansion remains and the cul-de-sac now contains a small development of modern houses.

On the path near Hitcham Road

Section 3 Taplow to Burnham

Distance: 2km   Time: 30 minutes

From Stockwells go up Berry Hill for about 150m and turn right, into Rectory Road. In a few minutes reach Taplow village green.

By the green is the Oak and Saw pub. Beside it is St Nicolas House, immediately after which you should turn right, along an earth path through trees. In a couple of minutes leave the trees and turn left on another path. In three minutes go through a kissing-gate and cross Boundary Road.

Do not go up the broad farm track. Instead, go through a staggered gate — which may be obscured by trees — and on to a narrow earth path with the hedgerow of Boundary Road Stables on your *left*. You now have a good view toward Burnham, with the tall chimneys of Slough Trading Estate beyond it.

Less than 10 minutes from Boundary Road, go through a staggered gate, cross Hitcham Road and go along a path into woods.

You soon pass under an old brick bridge and then follow a curiously sunken track. In places its banks are well above head-height and in summer the trees interleave to form a canopy overhead.

Soon the track takes you up a slope, then through three kissing-gates before reaching Lent Rise Road, on the edge of Burnham village. It will take you 10 minutes to get here from Hitcham Road.

Just north of Burnham there was a location for one of Gerry Anderson's later series, Secret Service, which featured the lovable but wacky Stanley Unwin. He played Father Stanley Unwin, outwardly a parish priest but in fact an agent for BISHOP, an especially covert branch of British Intelligence. (The scenes at his vicarage were filmed at Foxlea Manor on Dorneywood Road, unfortunately a couple of miles off our route.)

Unwin was the undisputed guru of gobbledygook, and Anderson thought that the American market would love his English eccentricity. But by that time Anderson had sold his company to TV magnate Lew Grade, and Grade took a different view.

At a pilot screening all went well until the point when Unwin, stopped by a policeman for speeding, said "Ah, yes, writey scribbly in your bookery, all uttery words speed of your penceload must defeat my eyebold."

In horror, Lew Grade jumped to his feet and shouted, "Cancel it!"

It was a decision that would lead to the closure of the studios.

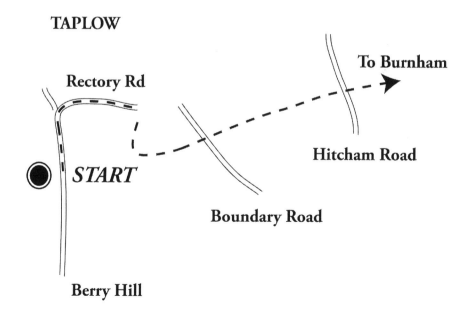

BURNHAM VILLAGE

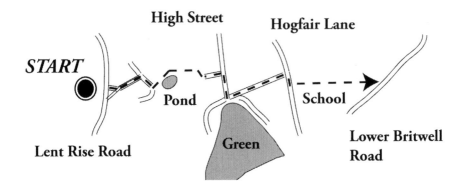

Section 4 *Burnham village to Burnham station*

Distance: 3.5km   Time: 50 minutes

Cross Lent Rise Road, go down Lent Green and in 50m turn left along Church Walk. Very soon come to a street of modern houses and at the far end of it turn right, down Lent Green Lane. After 50m go left, along a tarmac path with a duck-pond on your right. At the far end of the pond, at a five-way junction of tarmac paths, turn sharp right and go up to Church Street, passing St Peter's church on your right and the Old Five Bells pub on your left.

At the end of Church Street turn right into High Street. Soon turn left along the road that skirts the village green, and then immediately turn left (it feels like going straight ahead) along Lincoln Hatch Lane. Pass Burnham Electric Theatre and come to a T-junction with Hogfair Lane. Cross Hogfair Lane and go to the right, in the direction of Burnham Grammar School, but then almost immediately turn left on a bridleway alongside the school grounds. A 10-minute walk along the bridleway will bring you to Lower Britwell Road, where you leave Burnham and come into Slough.

Cross Lower Britwell Road. Keep straight on for a few minutes, following the pavement of Long Furlong Road, until you are at a dip in the road. Here turn right and go into a grassy park (Lammas Meadow). Follow an earth path for about three minutes, passing a basketball pitch, and come to Whittaker Road.

Almost directly across Whittaker Road you will see a small wood, just to the left of Littlebrook Avenue. It is Haymill Valley Nature Reserve, known locally as "The Millie".

The Millie

Near its right-hand corner is a metal kissing-gate. Go through it and keep straight on along an earth path. Uneven in places, and sometimes muddy, it follows a winding course but runs more or less parallel to Littlebrook Avenue. There are several forks to the left, but ignore them.

In under 10 minutes, when your path comes for the first time right up to the metal fence, behind a block of flats, leave the wood and go up to Littlebrook Avenue. Turn left and in about 100m keep straight ahead to go through a short alleyway between metal fences. Then cross Burnham Lane and Station Road and reach the driveway of Burnham railway station.

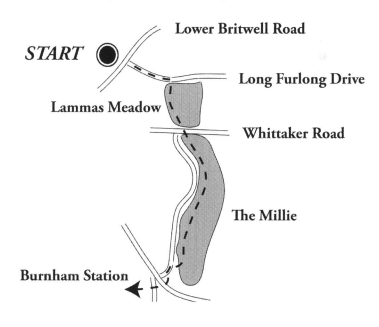

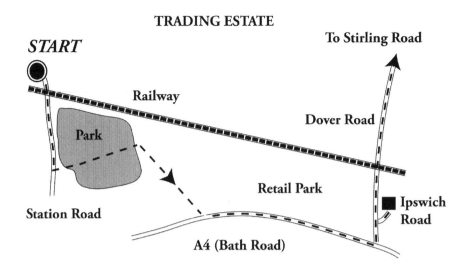

TRADING ESTATE

START

To Stirling Road

Railway

Dover Road

Park

Retail Park

Ipswich Road

Station Road

A4 (Bath Road)

Section 5   Burnham station via Ipswich Road to Stirling Road

Distance: 3km   Time: 45 minutes

Much of this section is unavoidably urban and trafficky.

Go down Station Road and through the railway arch. Then re-cross Station Road and continue alongside a hedge until you can turn left into Cippenham Recreation Ground. Go through this pleasant small park on a tarmac track and immediately beyond the far park boundary turn right on another tarmac track. At a staggered junction keep straight ahead and come in a few minutes to the busy A4 (Bath Road).

Turn left along the A4, passing the retail park (McDonald's, B&Q, etc.). Then cross Dover Road at the lights and turn left along it. Almost immediately come to a junction with Ipswich Road. The red-brick gable wall of the old AP Films studio is facing you and is now home to a tyre-fitting company.

AP Films moved here in 1960. Their first project was Four Feather Falls. Then came Supercar which started shooting in September 1960. Fireball XL5 followed in 1962.

The puppets became more lifelike and the special effects more convincing. Inside the studio, cloud-vistas would sweep endlessly past on roller-driven canvas while explosives brought down miniature cities. Outside, missiles and sundry spacecraft would hover at the back of the building, startling passers-by.

The Ipswich Road building today

The special effects people became very, very good. One of them later took charge of the "FX" on James Bond films; another worked on Kubrick's 2001, A Space Odyssey.

In 1964, having outgrown the Ipswich Road premises the company moved to bigger studios in Stirling Road, our next stop.

Continue north along Dover Road and cross the railway. In a few minutes turn right at traffic lights into Buckingham Avenue. In a couple of minutes turn left into Fairlie Road, then turn right into Edinburgh Avenue.

Here you pass a power station, with tall chimneys to your right and cooling towers to your left. Just after the cooling towers turn left into Stirling Road, a cul-de-sac. At its peak the "Anderson" company, by then owned by Lew Grade and renamed Century 21 Organisation, occupied most of the buildings in this road. The main office was in the buildings now used by Sovrin Plastics.

Stingray was the first production in the new studios. Then in 1964 came the hugely popular Thunderbirds.

Soon they were doing hour-long episodes of Thunderbirds, including one based on giant alligators. It was "one of the best," Sylvia Anderson wrote in her autobiography, adding that they used live crocodiles — but failing to add that the reptiles were given hefty electric shocks to make them perform.

The Ipswich Road building today

More humane, and even more surreal, was the feature film Thunderbirds Are Go! which included a floridly bizarre dream-sequence involving Cliff Richard and the Shadows.

In 1967 filming started on Captain Scarlet and the Mysterons. Joe 90 came next. But neither series matched the earlier success of Thunderbirds. Gerry Anderson judged it was time for a different approach, with live action rather than puppets.

And that is where Stanley Unwin enters the story, with The Secret Service. As we have seen, things ended badly. The studios closed in 1969.

After looking round Stirling Road, make your way to the A4 (Bath Road). The quickest way is to come back to Edinburgh Avenue and turn left along it.

Then turn right, into Liverpool Road. Near a row of shops keep straight ahead, to join Leigh Road. After crossing the railway come to the A4 (Bath Road). There is a bus stop about 150m to your left.

WALK 2

The Empty Quarter

Starting at the eastern extremity of the borough, this route visits three attractive villages: Colnbrook (which is part of Slough) and Horton and Wraysbury (which are not). Historical interest comes from Colnbrook's (alleged) lurid past, the site of John Milton's house, a ruined Benedictine priory and an ancient yew tree with pagan associations. At one point you are also close to an island on which some people believe the Magna Carta was sealed.

The route is almost wholly within the Colne Valley Regional Park, and mainly offers a pleasant mix of pasture, wood and lakeland. However it is not well-trodden and you will often be quite alone, hence our title. You should, however, see and hear a lot of birdlife — at any time of year, but especially in the winter months when large numbers of ducks come to the lakes, and flocks of geese and lapwings forage on the grassy meadows.

Distance: 16km.   *Time:* 4 hours.

Start/finish point: Colnbrook.

Transport to/from start/finish: No 81 bus from/to Slough bus station.

Surfaces: The route mainly follows earth paths which can be muddy in places. There are several kissing-gates, stiles at a rail crossing, and a short run of steps near the Ankerwycke Yew.

Facilities on the way: Colnbrook has shops and pubs. Horton has a shop and a pub. Wraysbury has pubs, shops and a café. Hythe End has a shop.

Can I shorten it? From Wraysbury you can take trains via Windsor to Slough. Or you can take a No 60 bus from Wraysbury to Slough (but note that the service is infrequent on Sundays).

Any unpleasant sections? The stage between Colnbrook and Horton goes under the Heathrow flight-path. The stage near Hythe End is alongside a road that can be busy at peak periods.

A NOTE ABOUT COLNBROOK

Colnbrook may prefer to be remembered as the birthplace of the Cox's Pippin apple, but that wholesome legacy always tends to be elbowed aside by the juicier fable about the Olde Ostrich Inn, whose onetime landlord reputedly murdered 60 of his guests. You can read about it in any book on local heritage. You can even join an all-night ghost hunt in the hope of befriending one of the victims (thirty-nine quid, credit-cards accepted).

The Most Haunted TV show visited the pub in 2002, its investigative team featuring a distinguished psychic medium who would later famously hold a televised *live séance* with the deceased pop-star Michael Jackson — and who now found "especially powerful emanations" in the ladies' toilet.

In their reportage, the investigators took the opportunity to increase the tally of alleged murders to 70, and they also concluded that the place was veritably bristling with psychic activity (which had increased recently, the landlord dutifully insisted, when the council started to dig up the road).

Unfortunately, psychic evidence notwithstanding, very little of the serial-killer story seems to be true.

The Ostrich Inn

It turns out that is a story that first emerged in 1602, in a novel by Thomas Deloney. Called The Pleasant Historie of Thomas of Reading, the novel contains all the elements of the tradition that survives today. A wealthy merchant named Thomas Cole stops at the inn for the night. The landlord named Jarman, assisted by his wife, plies him with strong drink then sends him off to bed, in a room with a specially-designed four-poster placed on top of a trap-door (the construction of which, it should be said, would have constituted a challenging DIY project in those days).

Presently Jarman pulls a lever that opens the trap-door and drops Cole into a vat of boiling liquid. Jarman dumps the body in the river Colne. Discovery of the murder leads to Jarman's confession of dozens of other killings, and he and his wife are hanged for their crimes.

It may be that Deloney's book is based on real events, but there is no evidence to support that view. On the contrary, The Pleasant Historie is a compendium of linked tales, each one as fanciful and overdrawn as the others. So if you wish to accept the Jarman material as fact, you should also be ready, for example, to accept the saga of Sir William Ferrers.

Ferrers "laid hard siege to the fort of the chastity" of one Faire Margaret, a servant, but without breaching her defences. Pressed to explain her reluctance to submit to his advances, Margaret confessed, "I will tell you: it is, sir, your ill-favoured great nose, that hangs sagging so lothsomely to your lips, that I cannot finde in my heart so much as to kisse you."

For a second opinion the distraught man consulted his medic. "'With reverence I may speake it" said the physician, "to tell the truth, and avoid flattery, I never saw a more misshapen nose so foule to sight."

The account of the ingenious way in which the doctor convinces the knight that his nose has again "come into some reasonable proportion" is well worth reading.

And so is the sad ending of Faire Margaret's tale. Her comeliness by and by wins the heart of the duke, Robert, even though he knows a nobleman should ne'er wed a humble serving-girl. But the union is angrily vetoed by Robert's brother, the king, who puts out Robert's eyes and throws him in prison. "Trust me, I do now detest life, worse than a goat doth hate Basill", Robert declares miserably as Margaret betakes herself to a nunnery — though not before, rather late in the day, announcing that she is in reality the daughter of the Earle of Shrewsburie and is thus herself of noble blood.

It's all great stuff. But to treat it as historical fact is to take a big risk.

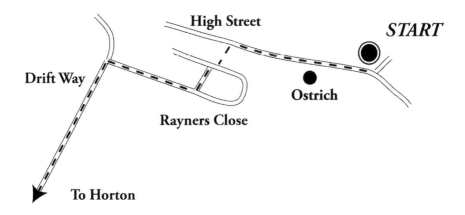

Section 1 Colnbrook to Horton

Distance: 2.5km   Time: 35 minutes

Get off the bus at the Old George pub and walk back (west) along the High Street, soon passing the Ostrich Inn, on the other side of the road.

The Ostrich claims to be the third oldest pub in England, dating back to 1106. But the original building was destroyed by fire and the present one was built around 1500.

Cross the road at a zebra crossing, continue west, then very soon turn left down an alley beside a doctor's surgery and come to a residential road. In quick succession turn right, left and then right, and go along to the end of Rayners Close. Here turn left down Drift Way and at the end of it join a bridleway signed "Colne Valley Way".

You are now on an unromantic section of our walk. You are directly below Heathrow's flight path. There are gravel workings on your right.

On your left there may be a sturdy metal fence separating you from a large arable field. It is part of the "two miles of security fencing" that the local farmer sometimes feels obliged to erect. When interviewed in 2012 by the Windsor & Eton Express, he said he suffered "on average a crime a day" — a mix of fly-tipping, thefts of vehicles and tools, and people on motorbikes damaging his crops.

About 10 minutes after joining the bridleway, reach Foundry Lane and follow it along to Stanwell Road. Here your route goes to the right and soon comes to Horton village.

But before going into Horton, make a short detour to your left. Less than 50m from Foundry Lane you reach the gates of Berkyn Manor Farm where a plaque says "John Milton, poet, lived here 1632-1638". Unfortunately nothing remains of the old house in which he stayed.

On the way into Horton, soon after the Five Bells pub, you pass St Michael's church, where Milton's mother Sara is buried. The church has a stained glass window commemorating Milton's best-known work, Paradise Lost, though the poet did not publish that work until 1667, almost 30 years after leaving Horton. Perhaps his main work dating from the Horton years is a pastoral poem called Lycidas.

When you have just gone past the triangular road intersection, at the centre of Horton village, turn sharp left into Park Lane.

St Michael's church, Horton

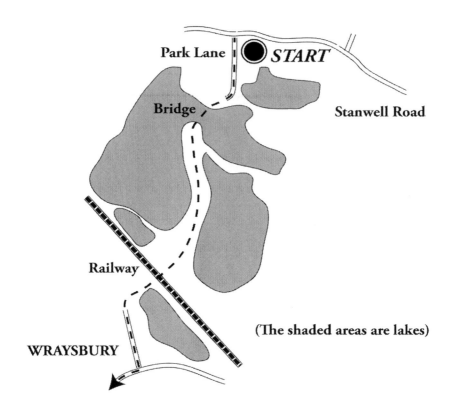

Park Lane ● *START*

Bridge

Stanwell Road

Railway

WRAYSBURY

(The shaded areas are lakes)

Section 2 Horton to Wraysbury

Distance: 2.5km   Time: 35 minutes

Go to the end of Park Lane, passing boarding kennels after a bend, and join
an earth path. Very soon a footbridge takes you over a wide channel between
two angling lakes that have been created on the site of former gravel workings.
(The area surrounding Wraysbury was extensively excavated over a period of
about 50 years during the twentieth century.)

It's worth pausing to take a look in the water — there are some very big fish
around here.

One angler recently pulled a mirror carp weighing 53lbs from the lake on
your left, which is called *Kingsmead One*. In the other lake, *Horton Island*, it
is estimated that there are several hundred fish that each weigh around 30lbs.
The waters in this area are said to be among the best in the country and
people pay up to £1,000 per year to fish in them.

Continue through woods and in less than 10 minutes reach a wide gravel road. Go straight along it for five minutes until you come to the London to Windsor railway line (which is on the far side of a row of trees).

At the trees, turn left and then almost immediately go right and cross the railway line at the authorised crossing. (There are stiles at both sides, with warning notices telling you to stop, look and listen.)

An earth path then brings you in five minutes to the edge of Wraysbury village, at the end of Douglas Lane. Go down Douglas Lane. At the far end of it turn right, along Station Road, and in a few minutes reach the Perseverance pub, a nice old place with a beer garden at the back.

Immediately before the pub turn right, on to a short tarmac road called The Green. At its end, take a path past a duck-pond. After the pond, if you look to your left, you will see a reconditioned windmill.

Now you reach the continuation of the road called The Green. Follow it, soon going alongside a park and cricket ground.

Wraysbury Lake

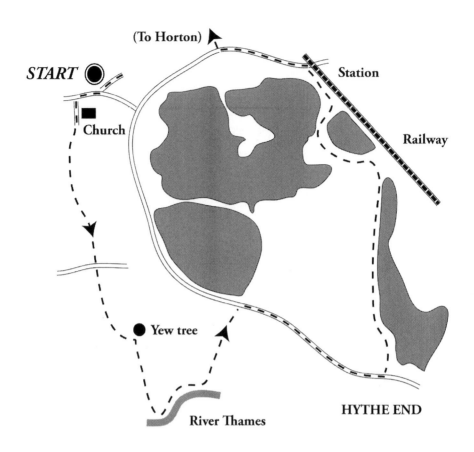

START

(To Horton)

Station

Church

Railway

Yew tree

River Thames

HYTHE END

Section 3 Wraysbury to Ankerwycke Yew

Distance: 2km   Time: 30 minutes

At the end of The Green turn right into Windsor Road and cross it. Pass the fine old house called The Grange then turn left down St Andrews Lane and continue into St Andrews churchyard. Follow a gravel path round the church then turn left on a slab path and leave the churchyard through a kissing-gate.

Take a faint path across the grassy field and in about 70m go through a kissing-gate to join an earth path which has a ditch on its left. At times this path goes among trees, at times across pastures.

In about 10 minutes you come to Magna Carta Lane near its junction with a residential street called Mere Road. Magna Carta Island, possibly the site of the sealing of the Magna Carta in 1215, is just a few minutes' walk down the lane, to your right, and is linked to the "mainland" by a small bridge.

However, as there is no public access to Magna Carta Island, you should go straight across Magna Carta Lane (kissing-gate on either side) and follow a path straight ahead, across grassy pastures. You are now on Ankerwycke Estate, which is managed by the National Trust.

Five minutes from Magna Carta Lane, go over a ditch on a footbridge. Then turn left and head for a kissing-gate about 70m away, at the edge of a wood. Go through the gate and follow an earth path which soon reaches a T-junction. Turn right and very soon come to a plaque which says that the tree facing you is the Ankerwycke Yew, "one of the Great British Trees". It is at least 2,000 years old.

The trunk sometimes has ivy wreaths or little sheaves of straw attached to it. This may be the work of the Ankerwycke Circle, a group of sixty or so pagans that regularly convenes here for rituals. "Picture this," they say, describing their outdoor meetings, "candles flickering, incense smoke curling up into the trees, drums gently beating and the chants begin as we prepare to remember those who have gone before."

Their indoor sessions, possibly less atmospheric, are held once a month in a room at the Conservative Club in nearby Staines. (Ring the bell and ask for Eileen's group, the website says.)

Ankerwycke estate

Section 4 Ankerwycke Yew to Wraysbury

Distance 4km   Time 60 mins

From the yew tree's plaque keep straight on and in about 50m come to a path junction.

To the right, only a few metres away, are the ruins of the 12th-century Benedictine Priory of St Mary. But your route goes left and in two minutes you turn left again at a path junction and go down half a dozen stone steps. Very soon you leave the wood through a kissing-gate and come into a pasture. Here turn left and head for another kissing-gate about 50m away. Go through it, cross a footbridge and come in about 50m to the River Thames.

Turn left on the riverside path. In less than five minutes the path turns sharp left, away from the river, and soon goes through a kissing-gate, with the residential Hythe End Estate on your right. In under 10 minutes you come to Staines Road, beside a house with a double-decker bus parked inexplicably in its back garden. (Another house along the road used to display a full-size human skeleton in the front window but, alas, it no longer does so.)

Carefully cross Staines Road and turn right. In 10 minutes pass through Hythe End village and just after a bridge over the Colne Brook, turn left down a short flight of steps into the grounds of "Wraysbury Lakes".

Now follow an attractive tree-fringed grassy path northward, with the Colne Brook on your left and a lake on your right.

In about 15 minutes you come to the London to Windsor railway line. You can cross it here, at an authorised crossing, and then turn left on a footpath that leads to Station Road, but the way is often overgrown with nettles.

It may be easier not to cross the railway, but to stay on your grassy path and follow it round to the left. In less than two minutes it takes you across the Colne Brook by a hefty footbridge, after which you immediately turn right on another grassy path. It takes you in under 10 minutes to Wraysbury station. Go left, up to Station Road, and turn left along it. In about five minutes turn right, into Douglas Lane.

From here return to Colnbrook by reversing your outward route.

WALK 3

The Way of Tubal Cain

This route follows mainly pleasant pathways, goes through two parks and three nature reserves and ends in fine woodland. So it works well simply as a nice walk. But if your concept of *heritage* has room for the quirky, it can also serve as a kind of remembrance of a Slough resident who, in the 1960s, was a guiding light in the neo-pagan movement and who has been called "one of the most important witches of the modern era". It's an uncommon sort of epithet.

Robert Cochrane, born Roy Leonard Bowers, lived in a council house in Britwell — not the most romantic neighbourhood in Britain, nor even in Slough. But in spite of his unexceptional surroundings Cochrane claimed descent from a centuries-long line of witches, some of whom had been executed for their beliefs. And though he got his living as a typeface designer, he also laid claim to an exotic CV that included one stint as a bargeman and another as a blacksmith.

It was the blacksmithing that suggested the name for his coven, the Clan of Tubal Cain. For in the book of Genesis (4:22) Tubal Cain — son of Lamech and Zilla — was the world's first metal-worker, a man who rose to fame as "an instructer of every artificer in brass and iron". Cochrane's Clan would sometimes meet in his house, and sometimes up the road in Burnham Beeches. This walk, more or less, links these two locations.

Distance: 7km.   *Time:* 2 hours.
Start point: Burnham station.   *Finish point:* Farnham Common.
Transport to start: Train or No 1B bus from Slough.
Transport from end: Bus No X74 to Slough bus station (once an hour, Monday to Saturday; once every 2 hours on Sunday.)
Surfaces: Mainly earth paths, rough in places. There are two flights of steps in Section 1 and several stiles in Section 2.
Facilities on the way: There is a pub at Lynch Hill. In Burnham Beeches there is a café with toilets. Farnham Common has shops, pubs and public toilets.
Can I shorten it? Section 1 works well enough as an out-and-back route.
Any unpleasant sections? The road-crossing at Farnham Lane can be tricky.

Section 1 Burnham railway station to Farnham Lane

Distance: 2km   Time: 30 minutes

From Burnham Station come out on to Station Road, go left for 50m and then carefully cross both Station Road and Burnham Lane. Once across turn left and then almost immediately go right, along a short alley between metal fences. It takes you to Littlebrook Avenue. Keep straight on for 100m until you reach the block of flats — on your right — numbered 155-177. Behind the building go through a gate in a metal fence and into the woods known locally as The Millie, a nature reserve.

Go left along an earth path that runs roughly parallel to the fence and brings you in under 10 minutes to Whittaker Road.

Here, on Whittaker Road, you are close to Tomlin Road, where Robert Cochrane had his home, and you can make the short detour if you want. It's about 250m along to your right and then up to the left.

30

If you like your coven-masters to dwell in remote cottages or Gothic mansions you'll be disappointed. Nevertheless, this is where Cochrane, with his wife, young son, Mynah bird and cat, lived for seven years until 1966. All the houses are in the same style, so there is no need to give a precise address. And for the sake of the current residents it's best not to. In the 1960s the house allegedly had a "nature spook". Cochrane called it Tomkins, and it was a noisy creature that would emit a pinging sound as midnight drew near. The present occupants probably blame it on the central heating and it would be a kindness to let them continue in that belief.

From the Millie's gate, cross Whittaker Road then go into a grassy park called Lammas Meadow. Follow an earth path along the left-hand side of the park. After three minutes cross Long Furlong Drive and go down a flight of steps into Lynch Hill Park. Keep straight ahead on an earth path and at the far end of the park go straight across Lynch Hill Lane and into Cocksherd Wood.

Follow an earth path through the wood. The path soon runs alongside a metal fence, and when the fence stops you should keep straight ahead for 50m until you reach the end of a little clearing. Here turn right, soon go up a long flight of wooden steps and two minutes later come a gate, at Farnham Lane.

Cochrane's coven was reputedly well-versed in herbal lore, "the old leaf-language", and it is likely that he came to both the Millie and Cocksherd Wood to gather willow-bark and pine-sap for incense, and to collect less innocent narcotics like belladonna that could be employed to induce trance-like states.

The Millie

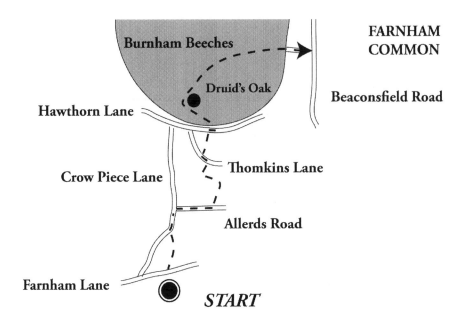

FARNHAM
COMMON

Burnham Beeches

Druid's Oak

Hawthorn Lane

Beaconsfield Road

Crow Piece Lane

Thomkins Lane

Allerds Road

Farnham Lane

START

Section 2 Farnham Lane to Burnham Beeches

Distance: 3km   Time: 45 minutes

Now go straight across Farnham Lane. You are near a bend made more perilous by hurrying drivers who seem to have incompletely grasped the concept of speed limits. Take care! Once across, go along Crow Piece Lane, a bridleway that climbs gently uphill. In about five minutes you come to a tarmac road. Walk along it for just a few paces and then go right, on to a public footpath that runs parallel to the road and is tightly squeezed between a hedge and a fence-railing.

After about 200m your path turns right, and now runs alongside Allerds Road. In a further 300m it crosses the road and goes into pleasant pastures. The signpost here may direct you over a barbed-wire fence and through a field full of horses. But ignore it and stay on the obvious path which almost traces three sides of a square around the field before bringing you to a tarmac road (Thompkins Lane).

Go left along Thompkins Lane for 150m until you can join a public footpath going off to the right. It goes over a stile, then along the right-hand side of a small grassy pasture. Then there is another stile and another pasture. And then there is yet another stile, which takes you to a tarmac road. This is Hawthorn Lane, which is on the perimeter of Burnham Beeches.

Go right for 150m until you reach a car park intended for visitors to the Beeches. Enter the car park and then go out at its far left-hand corner, taking a path that goes immediately into trees and comes in a few minutes to the Middle Pond. At the pond, turn left on to a broad path and follow it for 200m. Then leave the path to go across a grassy area on your right and come in about 50m to the 700-year-old Druid's Oak, beside a traffic-free road called Lord Mayors Drive.

(To end the walk, turn right, on to Lord Mayors Drive and go along it for about 15 minutes, passing a café and then the grassy expanse of East Burnham Common. Just after the common, cross Bedford Drive and go straight ahead, along Beeches Road. When you reach the main road through Farnham Common village (Beaconsfield Road) turn right. The bus stop is about 400m down this road, on the left.)

Robert Cochrane took a serious approach to the *Old Craft* and once described it as "a mystical religion with a puritanical attitude". A recurring theme in his writings is a contempt for the thrill-seekers who come to modern witchcraft for esoteric chant-fests and sky-clad romps in the dew: "Nudism, sex and free beer". Nevertheless he was partial to a bit of ritual and — together with his coven, all in hooded black robes — he would resort when the calendar was auspicious to this ancient beech forest.

One meeting has been vividly described by a guest-member of the coven. Inside a circle traced on the ground a fire was lit and a cauldron placed over it. The men processed around the fire, chanting and thrusting their knives into the cauldron. The women held aloft a dish, representing the Grail, and dipped it in the cauldron whose contents were then scattered using a sword. Then everyone went into a smaller circle and danced widdershins (anticlockwise) until "the Maid went into a trance and made a prophecy and a working known as Summoning the Spirit was performed".

Such rituals, which continued even after Cochrane's death, must have been something to behold. And I like to think that they were indeed beheld, and that they help to explain the sinister status the Beeches enjoys among modern conspiracy-theorists, notably David Icke.

Icke says he once met a woman who claimed that she was the wife of the "Warden" of Burnham Beeches and who also claimed that her husband was a Satanist. Although she lived "as a prisoner" she was compassionately allowed out to walk the dog on a regular basis, and one night she saw lights.

Creeping forward, she came upon a circle of robed people, chanting, and she thought she recognised among them Ted Heath, who was then Prime Minister.

"And she went on to tell me," Icke said, "that while she's watching this ritual, suddenly Heath transforms into a reptile figure [and] grows about two feet."

Perhaps lacking the time, or the ambition, to seek for corroborative evidence, Icke went right ahead and publicised the alleged woman's alleged account. And it has become an important element in his theory that planet Earth has been colonised — and is controlled — by the Anunnaki, a shape-shifting reptilian species from the Draco constellation.

Icke's theory could of course be right. But the Beeches on a dark night can be an eye-deceiving place. And there's just a chance that the group that his informant encountered was not a rocket-load of reptoids down from Draco, but a car-load of witches up from Slough.

I think Robert Cochrane would have liked that version of the story. But we'll never know. He committed suicide at the summer solstice in 1966, ingesting a cocktail of belladonna, hellebore and Librium. It took him nine days to die.

Some believe he killed himself as a sacrificial offering, for the good of the Clan. Others say it was the result of depression brought on when his wife, provoked by his openly adulterous behaviour, walked out. The coroner, leaving the specifics unresolved, simply recorded a verdict of "suicide whilst the balance of the mind was disturbed".

Crow Piece Lane

34

WALK 4

The Old Way

This walk pays homage to the writer Susan Cooper, who was educated at Slough High School — when it was located on Twinches Lane. A prolific author, now in her eighties and settled in the USA, she is best known for a sequence of five novels published between 1965 and 1977. Aimed at young teenagers they recount a series of epic struggles between the forces of the Light and the Dark, and weave together Arthurian legend, folklore, witchcraft and sorcery.

The second of the five stories, The Dark is Rising, is set near Cooper's childhood home. The main character, young Will Stanton, lives in the fictional village of Huntercombe (based on Dorney village). His dad works as a jeweller in Eton and the family goes shopping in Slough. Some of the outdoor action takes place on Huntercombe Lane and some on Oldway Lane (both real by-ways). Other outdoor locations are the River Thames and Dorney Common.

Much of the indoor action is set in Huntercombe Manor (based on Dorney Court) and in the real-life church of St James the Less, which is on the edge of Dorney village.

This walk links all these places. And it adds a medieval site at Cippenham as well as distant views of Windsor Castle, both of which were important to Susan Cooper when she was growing up.

"Things like that," she has said, "give a sense of layers and layers of time, and of the stories that stick to those layers and develop through them ... It's a great legacy for a writer."

Unfortunately, time's most recent layers have rather compromised the mythic ambience of the area, and the walker now needs to contend with a motorway, a housing estate that is not everywhere lovely, a supermarket and a sewage processing plant. But apart from all that ... well, surprisingly the route is a good one, and it keeps as much as possible to pleasant paths and lanes.

Distance: 15km.   *Time:* 3.75 hours.

Start/finish point: St Andrew's Lane bus-stops on A4 (Bath Road) at Cippenham, just before the M4 motorway spur for Junction 7.

Transport to/from start: Number 75/76 bus from/to Slough bus station.

Surfaces: The route starts and finishes on tarmac. On the way down from the first motorway crossing there is a steep ramp with some steps. After that the route follows earth and grit paths. There is a narrow, awkward footbridge at Dorney Common. On the Jubilee River there are swing gates.

Facilities on the way: Dorney has a pub and a garden centre with café. Near the end of the walk Asda's supermarket has a fast-food cafe.

Can I shorten it? You can miss out the Thames Path. After seeing round Dorney village (Section 2), retrace your steps to the Jubilee River and turn right, along the riverside bridleway and follow it for 1.5km until you reach a weir. Then you can rejoin our main route in Section 4.

Any unpleasant sections? The first part of Oldway Lane runs alongside the M4 approach. Section 2 goes for a few minutes on a path between the motorway and a sewage plant.

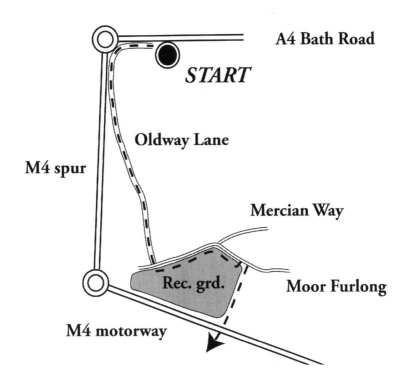

A4 Bath Road

START

Oldway Lane

M4 spur

Mercian Way

Rec. grd.

Moor Furlong

M4 motorway

Oldway Lane climbing to cross the M4

Section 1   A4 (Bath Road) to M4 motorway crossing

Distance: 2km   Time: 30 minutes

Get off the bus at St Andrew's Way. Walk west along the residential part of
Bath Road and stay on it when it soon bends to the left to join Oldway Lane.
Sometimes called Tramps' Alley in Cooper's book, and a place where rooks
flapped, *signs* were shown and diverse other weird things happened, Oldway
Lane is today a service-road that runs prosaically between the motorway spur
and the back-gardens of a row of houses.

In five minutes keep straight on at a path crossing and in another minute turn
right to go along a residential road still called Oldway Lane. At the end of it,
cross Mercian Way and go into Mercian Recreation Ground.

Go left along a tarmac track until you come to the corner of the park. Here at
a swing gate go out on to Moor Furlong and then immediately turn right, and
once again join Oldway Lane — which is now a bridleway — and follow it
over the M4 motorway.

From the bridge you get a distant view of Windsor Castle, and a close one of
Slough sewage treatment works.

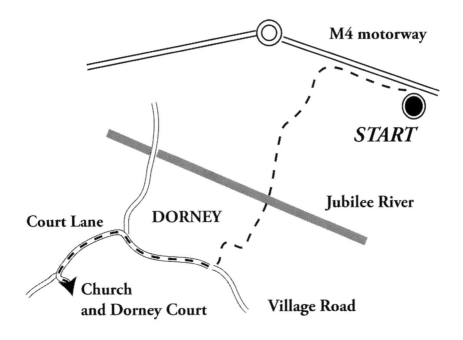

Section 2 Motorway crossing to Dorney village

Distance: 2.5km   Time: 35 minutes excluding coffee stop

Once across the motorway turn right, down a ramp and join an earth path between the motorway and a metal fence. In a few minutes turn left into trees and soon re-emerge at a footbridge. The path now crosses a field at an angle and heads for another footbridge about 100m away.

Immediately after this second footbridge you reach a path-crossing. Turn right, on a footpath that soon bends to the left and then goes straight ahead between two hedgerows. By now you will have been walking for over 30 minutes and, perhaps for the first time, you will feel that you are in attractive countryside.

Keep straight on and soon cross the Jubilee River on two bridges, the first over reed-beds, the second over the river proper. Sign-boards will tell you that you are in Dorney Wetlands.

Now continue across a wide bridleway and go straight along a gravel track. In 50m go through a swing-gate into a farm field; your path then continues between two wire fences. At the far side of the field turn right and in 100m turn left on a public footpath between high wooden fences. Very soon you emerge on the main road through Dorney. It is called Village Road.

Dorney is Cooper's "Huntercombe" and if you're a fan you will enjoy trying to locate the Stanton's house, the old shop, the smithy, etc. Be prepared for some difficulty, for Cooper used the village as a general inspiration rather than an exact template. The most straightforward location is "Huntercombe Manor", owned by the spookily enigmatic Miss Greythorne. It is based on real-life Dorney Court. The wood near Dorney Court is the fictional "Rooks Wood". Close to Dorney Court is the church of St James the Less which also features strongly in the story.

Without crossing Village Road, turn right and walk through Dorney village. You pass several delightful 17th century cottages in the Tudor style. In five minutes you come out of the village and can cross Village Road at a traffic island and then turn left into Court Lane. There is no footway on your side of Court Lane, so cross to the other side. Then cross back in about 50m and go down the driveway signposted for Dorney Court Kitchen Garden. In about 200m you reach a garden centre with a pleasant café. On the way you get a good, if distant, view of Dorney Court.

The café is a friendly but cultured sort of place, in which you are likely to hear Vivaldi on the music system and to read in the toilets quotations from Thoreau. ("Beware any enterprise that requires a new set of clothes.")

Dorney Court — seen on an open day

Section 3 Dorney village to Dorney Common

Distance: 6km   Time: 1 hour 30 minutes

When it is time to leave the café, return to Court Drive, cross it and turn left. In about three minutes re-cross the road and go down a short road with the church of St James the Less at the end of it. Huddled in a tiny churchyard it is a nice old building with a squat red-brick tower edged with weathered stone. Above the low main door is carved the date 1661. It is hard to suppress the thought that if Cooper had written her fantasy books in that year, the church people would have burned her at the stake.

After seeing the church, come back to Court Lane and turn left alongside it on an earth path. In two minutes turn left into the grounds of Dorney Rowing Lake on a public footpath that runs parallel to the main driveway.

Two minutes after entering the Lake grounds, go to the right, across the driveway, and join a gravel track signed "Maidenhead". In just under 10 minutes you reach the bank of the river Thames, opposite Bray Marina. Turn left along the Thames Path and follow the river downstream.

You now have about 40 minutes' riverbank walking. The route is pleasant and leafy and straightforward. On the way, Cooper fans can try to identify the island that features dramatically near the end of her book.

James the Less church

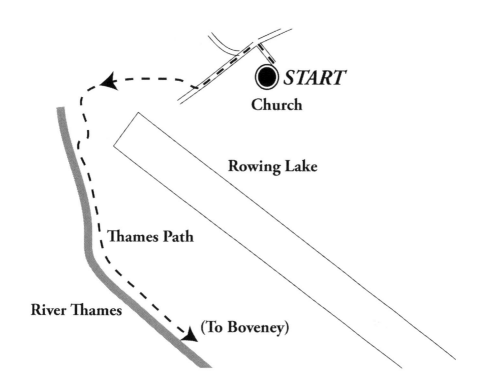

START

Church

Rowing Lake

Thames Path

River Thames

(To Boveney)

A NOTE ABOUT SUSAN COOPER

Susan Cooper was born in 1935 and lived in Westlands Avenue (just to the west of the M4 spur). She attended Slough High School, in those days on Twinches Lane, and became Head Girl in 1952. After school she went to Oxford University and then had seven "rapturous" years as a journalist at the Sunday Times where she worked alongside Ian Fleming. Away from their day-jobs both were writing novels, Fleming heading for riches and fame with James Bond.

Cooper's success was less meteoric, but she found a publisher for Over Sea, Under Stone, a charmingly old-fashioned yarn about plucky middle-class children who call their parents Mother and Father and use expressions like "I say!" "Splendid!" and "Gosh!" On holiday in Cornwall, assisted by craggy and mysterious Great-Uncle Merry, they find an ancient map whose riddles the oldest child helps unravel, using his knowledge of Latin grammar. *Don't you see? It's the ablative case!*

The novel is unmistakably the work of a Head Girl. But it laid a solid foundation for the five-book sequence, and the other four are much less conventional.

After walking on the Thames Path for about 40 minutes you pass a slipway near the buildings of Dorney Lake, then reach the little old church of St Mary Magdalene, which sits by a patch of grass just back from the river.

Here you leave the river and go down an earth path just to the left of the church. In 150m you come to the tarmac access road for Boveney Lock. Turn right along it for about 100m, then turn left on to an earth footpath. It goes alongside a large arable field, with Eton Wick village visible beyond it.

Follow this path to the corner of the field and stay on it when it turns right and soon brings you to a footbridge over the Cress Brook. (You might not see the bridge until you are very close to it.) It is a narrow footbridge with two awkward steps on each side. Go across it and be thankful that the Brook is normally a shallow stream. In The Dark is Rising it becomes a rushing torrent above which storms rage and warlocks grapple.

Once across the bridge you reach Dorney Common. Turn obliquely right, on a grassy path that will take you in under five minutes to the point where Common Road crosses a cattle grid on its way into Eton Wick village.

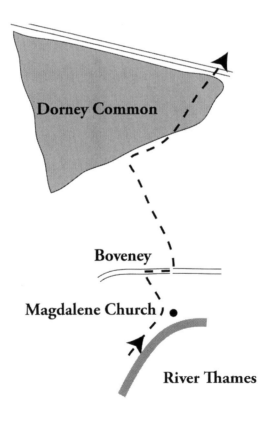

Crossing the footbridge to Dorney Common

Section 4 Dorney Common to A4 Bath Road

Distance: 4.5km   Time: 1 hour 10 minutes

Do not go into Eton Wick, but instead cross Common Road and follow a grassy path alongside the brook — a favourite haunt of herons and a place where you may see kingfishers. In five minutes you reach the northeast corner of the Common and leave it through a kissing-gate. Your path goes up a short slope and at the top you can see the Jubilee River, just ahead.

Turn right and go down to a weir, then keep going on a broad bridleway with the river just on your left. Soon go through a kissing-gate and turn left to cross the river on a footbridge. Your path becomes a tarmac road that goes through bollards then bears right at Wood Lane before climbing to cross the M4 motorway. Just after the motorway, to your right, is the Asda supermarket.

For a nice detour, continue down Wood Lane for about 200m and then turn right just after Asda, on to a tarmac path that leads to Cippenham Moat. A plaque explains that this site, a scheduled monument, is probably the remains of a 13th Century palace owned by Richard, Earl of Cornwall. On the western side, close to Wood Lane, you can see where a causeway once crossed the moat.

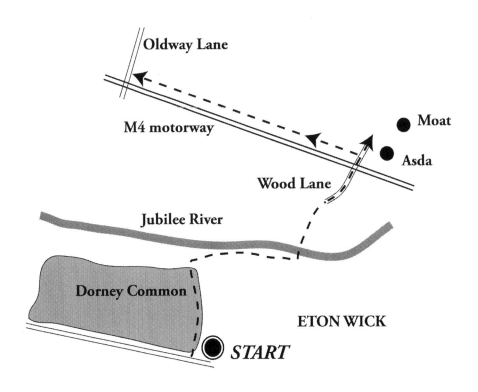

Oldway Lane

M4 motorway

Moat

Asda

Wood Lane

Jubilee River

Dorney Common

ETON WICK

START

After the detour, retrace your steps to the M4 bridge. Do not re-cross it, but instead go down a ramp that is now on your right — ie, the opposite side from Asda.

The ramp takes you down to a gravel bridleway that runs parallel to the motorway. You will follow this bridleway for about 15 minutes, until you reach the motorway bridge you crossed at the end of Section 1. A wooden fence and a line of trees combine to cut down the road noise and this is a surprisingly nice stretch.

When you reach that familiar motorway bridge, turn right along Oldway Lane and retrace your outward route, through Mercian Recreation Ground and up the rest of Oldway Lane, to the A4 (Bath Road). Turn right along Bath Road and in 250m cross it at a controlled crossing. From the nearby stop you can catch a bus back to Slough bus station.

WALK 5

The Path of Glory

This route is based around Slough's literary associations, or some of them at least. As we saw in Walk 4, Susan Cooper gets a route to herself. Here we include Charles Dickens, Thomas Gray, John Milton, John King and Alduous Huxley — not a bad tally for a provincial town.

True to the spirit — if you like — of Thomas Gray, for whom *the paths of glory lead but to the grave*, we visit two churchyards, one cemetery and one crematorium. This brings an inescapable melancholy, so you might prefer to keep the walk for a bright sunny day.

Distance: 14km.   *Time:* 3.5 hours.

Start point: Herschel Park.   *Finish point:* Wexham Park Hospital.

Transport to start: Bus or train to central Slough then walk to Herschel Park.

Transport from end: Bus WP1 (Monday to Friday) or No 6 (every day) to Slough bus station.

Facilities on the way: There is a pub at the Red Cow roundabout. There are shops at Trelawney Avenue. Near St Mary's church, Langley, there is a pub. On Elliman Avenue there is a small general store.

Surfaces: From Herschel Park to the canal you mostly have tarmac tracks, except in and near Ditton Park where the tracks are mainly gravel. There are A-frame gates at Ditton Park, which is open only from 6am to 6pm (8pm in summer). The canal towpath is an earth path with several kissing-gates. From Elliman Avenue to the golf course you are again on tarmac paths.

Can I shorten it? You can stop at St Mary's church and catch a bus from Langley Road to central Slough, or walk to Langley station for a train. Or you can stop after the canal section and walk to central Slough.

Any unpleasant sections? There is some roadside walking on Elliman Avenue and again after the crematorium. For a short while the route goes through a golf course, immediately after which is a short section of badly-kept path.

We start at a half-timbered house called The Mere, which is often but incorrectly associated with Charles Dickens. It was formerly the home of the Bentley family publishers who indeed collaborated with Dickens. But it was built in 1887, by which time the collaboration had been over for fifty years and the writer was in his grave. There may be another link between Dickens and the borough — but we'll come to that soon.

Close to The Mere is St Laurence's church which has an association with Thomas Gray, possibly Britain's best-known poet. His fame is due to the Elegy Written in a Country Churchyard, published in 1750. It is, as the website of Stoke Poges Parish Council says, "one of the most popular and most frequently quoted poems in the English language". Stoke Poges has a legitimate interest, for the work was completed while Gray was living there and it has many local references. But it may also have reflected the poet's experience of St Laurence's church, which he would have known whilst a pupil at nearby Eton College. Its tower is often thought to have inspired these lines:

And all the air a solemn stillness holds …
Save that from yonder ivy-mantled tow'r
The moping owl does to the moon complain
Of such, as wand'ring near her secret bow'r,
Molest her ancient solitary reign.

The moping owl might nowadays complain about traffic roar from the M4 just down the road, but the churchyard is still a remarkably calm place and it is worth lingering a while.

The Mere

46

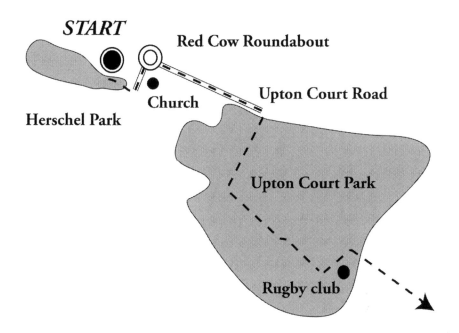

START

Red Cow Roundabout

Upton Court Road

Church

Herschel Park

Upton Court Park

Rugby club

Section 1 Herschel Park to Ditton Park

Distance: 2.5km   Time: 35 minutes

Begin at Herschel Park's east entrance. For the best views of The Mere (now occupied by the National Foundation for Educational Research) walk up the lower of the two paths that climb into the nature park area. After you have looked at the house, cross Datchet Road, turn left and in about 100m go into St Laurence's churchyard for a look at the exterior of "Slough's oldest building". If you go on an open day you can also see inside the church.

When you are ready to move on, turn right, along Upton Court Road. In 400m turn right again, into Upton Court Park and go down the main drive. At the bottom of the hill, just beyond a line of trees, turn left on a wide tarmac track. In a few minutes go left at a Y-junction and soon reach Slough Rugby Club. Turn left on to a wide tarmac drive and very soon, just after crossing a stream, turn right along a gravel track beside the boundary of Slough Cricket Club. In 10 minutes you will reach Ditton Park.

On this section you can consider the possibility that Charles Dickens and a young and pretty actress called Nelly Ternan for a time habitually walked this way, bound for Datchet railway station, from where the writer would journey into London.

For there is some evidence — though not much — that Dickens rented a house on Slough High Street from 1866 to 1867, that Miss Ternan lived in it and that Dickens frequently visited her. (The house is said to have been Elizabeth Cottage, which had been occupied by the astronomer Caroline Herschel a half-century earlier — see Walk 6),

This so-called Dickens Scandal is an old story and over the years it has become encrusted with a great deal of prurient tat, goss for graduates. In the more florid versions the couple at one time moved to Paris to have a love-child (because Paris was far from the prying eyes of London), but then pitched up in Slough some years later to have another one (because Slough was *handy* for London). The alleged babies conveniently died before the Registrars of Births, Marriages and Deaths had time to deploy.

In 2013 a feature film called The Invisible Woman attempted to re-stir the pot. Ralph Fiennes played Dickens and Felicity Jones was Nelly. The film was based on a Claire Tomalin book of the same name, published in 1991, in which fact and speculation seemed to co-exist in homeopathic ratio. Mercifully the film flopped. One critic, intending to give praise, said it demonstrated a "finely calibrated poetic obliqueness that draws the viewer into the relationship's gradual unfolding". Which might have been rendered alternatively as, it was difficult to follow and slow.

Ditton Manor - seen on an open day

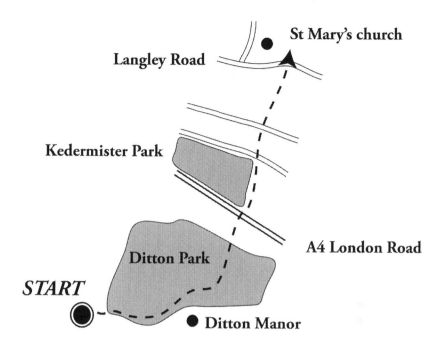

Section 2 Ditton Park to St Mary's Church, Langley

Distance: 2.5km   Time: 35 minutes

In Ditton Park, at an A-frame gate, you join a rougher gravel track and soon go past the squat towers of Ditton Manor. Built in 1817, it is now owned by Computer Associates. A few minutes beyond it, turn left on a tarmac road and soon leave the park at Cedar Way.

The A4 (London Road) is now less than 200m away, in front of you. Cross it at the lights, then go straight ahead on the tarmac track called Green Lane. In 10 minutes, after crossing two other roads, you will reach Langley Road.

There, your next footpath is directly across the road. Cross at the nearby lights and soon go into St Mary's churchyard. The churchyard and the adjacent almshouses are attractive and atmospheric and deserve a close look.

On your way from Ditton Park you may have been following in the footsteps of John Milton. From 1632 to 1638 he lived in Horton (see Walk 2). A scholarly man who crammed allusions to classical Rome and Greece into his verse, he would have needed to use a library. And a well-stocked one, the Kedermister Library, had existed since 1613 at St Mary's church. It would have been only an hour's walk from Horton.

Kedermister Library is still there and you can see it on a tour organised by the church. (Generally the tours take place on the afternoon of the first Sunday in each summer month — May to September. Details are posted on the church website at *www.langleymarish.com*.)

To get to the library you have to squeeze through the Kedermister family pew, which is screened from the main congregation by fretwork panels. The library itself is a small but strikingly impressive room in which massive leather-bound books are shelved behind illustrated panels. It's an atmospheric place, just the kind of setting you'd like to imagine for Milton, and a tradition has grown up that he did indeed come here during his Horton years.

But the evidence is inconclusive. One academic scholar, after reviewing the matter, offered this delightful assertion: "While the collateral persuasions are strong, the lack of consistent or even predominant fit between the Kedermister imprints and those referred to by Milton is a serious hurdle for the Kedermister hypothesis". (Poole, 2013.)

In other words: it's possible that Milton used the library, but we're not sure.

Almshouses beside St Mary's church

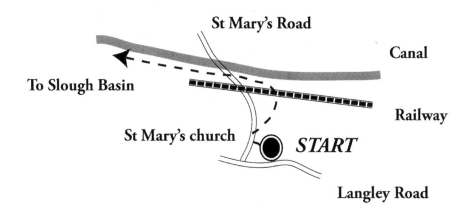

St Mary's Road

Canal

To Slough Basin

Railway

St Mary's church

START

Langley Road

Section 3   *St Mary's Church to Slough Basin*

Distance: 3.5km   Time: 50 minutes

Leave the churchyard by the St Mary's Road gate (opposite the Red Lion pub), turn right, along the pavement, and go past both almshouse buildings. Then turn right, on a tarmac footpath. Very soon, when you reach a patch of lawn, turn left on another tarmac footpath and come to Minster Way.

Turn left along Minster Way and soon come to its junction with Maryside. Here you will see a new footpath and cycleway, accessed by a flight of steps and a ramp.

Follow the footpath over a railway bridge, and come to a bridge over the Grand Union Canal. Don't cross it, but go down a ramp to the towpath and turn left, so that the water is on your right. Follow the towpath for about 30 minutes, to the end of the canal at Slough Basin.

Our next writer, John King, features this stretch of water in his novel Human Punk. Published in 2000, it is as different from Milton's work as it's possible to imagine. King fundamentally rejects the classical standpoint that Milton and, he claims, most other writers adopt, a standpoint he sees as irrelevant to working class people. Instead he champions other cultural forms, like the punk rock music that serves as background to his novel. Punk musicians, he says, "were the best writers, producing the sort of literature that dealt with our lives."

Human Punk is an unlovely fable, set mainly in Slough and peopled by school drop-outs, head-kicking street fighters, under-age drinkers who steal cars and drive them ten-pints drunk, and adults who brick the windows of neighbourhood shops, knock over factories, deal in dope and cocaine, and even commit murder.

The canal is a crucial location. Early in the story main character Joe Martin and his pal, Smiles, are beaten up and thrown into the water. Joe recovers but Smiles goes into a coma from which he emerges a broken soul headed for suicide. The rest of the novel is about how Joe copes with his friend's death.

People disagree about Human Punk. Some say it gives an authentic voice to a neglected *white-trash* segment of society. (King claims it is based on his own experience and proudly says he rarely does any research.) Others see it as a posturing attempt to romanticise a class of people that King himself is careful not to live among (preferring a desirable part of south London).

However, almost everyone dislikes the final part of the book. For as Joe Martin grows to adulthood he relentlessly voices a glib political view based on a slack and unfocussed hatred of The Establishment. This allows him to adopt a position where *any* antisocial act can be justified, because whatever is attacked can itself be portrayed as corrupt. In the process he becomes tedious and repellent.

It's therefore hard to empathise when Joe returns to the canal at the climax of the story. Gripped by crisis he swims naked out to the middle and ducks under the water. Down and down he goes, deeper and deeper, in one of King's signature two-page sentences, the tension increasing with every syllable.

Will he blow out his lungs and drown himself in a purifying act born of guilty despair? Will he?!

Well, it would be a surprise if he did. For even when newly built the canal had an average depth of only 1.15 metres, three foot six in the old money. And it's now so badly silted that the narrowboats can hardly get through.

But, to return to the real world, the waterway makes a good habitat for wildlife, and you might glimpse water voles, mallards and coots, and even a heron or two. Writing on the website *www.canoedaysout.com*, one canoeist reported seeing kingfishers and sparrow hawks and added "I've even seen a large turtle basking happily on a log that someone has obviously released when it grew too big."

The surroundings become more urban in character as you approach the Slough Basin, where the canal ends. There you can turn your attention to Alduous Huxley, whose Brave New World was one of the most influential novels of the twentieth century.

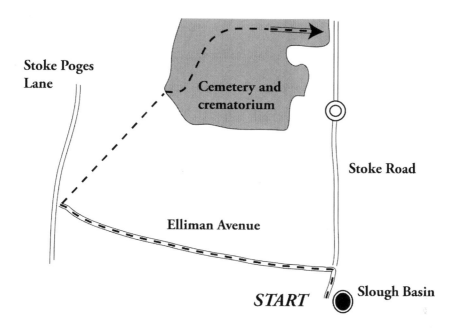

Stoke Poges Lane

Cemetery and crematorium

Stoke Road

Elliman Avenue

START Slough Basin

Section 4   Slough Basin to Slough Crematorium Gate

Distance: 1.5km   Time: 20 minutes

From the canal basin go through a kissing-gate and turn right on to Stoke Road. Cross it at the nearby traffic lights and go along Elliman Avenue for about 10 minutes, to its junction with Stoke Poges Lane. On the north side of the junction a footpath goes off obliquely to your right, between high metal railings. Go along it, with back-gardens to your left and sports fields to your right, and come in less than five minutes into Slough cemetery.

Turn left along the peripheral tarmac drive. In a couple of minutes, after the drive bends to the right, go left to the front of Slough crematorium. Follow the main driveway out of the crematorium grounds, to Stoke Road. Carefully cross this busy road, and turn left along the footway.

You have just gone past an important location in Alduous Huxley's story, though by the time of the novel, set in the 26th Century, the present modest structure has morphed into "the majestic buildings of the Slough Crematorium" which include four tall chimneys, each fitted with an elaborate filtering system. These are for phosphorous recovery, explains Henry Foster, a major character in the novel. And he proudly describes how the treatment processes achieve an impressive recovery of 98% of the available phosphorous, "more than a kilo and a half per adult corpse".

Path from Elliman Avenue to cemetery

Published in 1932 Brave New World portrays a society in which people are conditioned to know their place and in which, because real choice has been eliminated, unhappiness no longer exists. To make sure things stay that way the populace is given an unlimited supply of guilt-free promiscuous sex and of a drug called *soma*.

Huxley was educated at Eton College and returned there as a Master in 1917. Perhaps he was demonstrating an ingrained College prejudice when he opted to situate the nastier bits of his fictional society in Slough. But our northern neighbours share the harsh treatment, as we see when Henry Foster and his pneumatic squeeze, Miss Lenina Crowne, travel by helicopter to Stoke Poges, to play Obstacle Golf. From the air they look down on the grounds of the Internal and External Secretion Trust, where thousands of cattle produce the raw materials for "the great factory at Farnham Royal".

It's interesting to read Huxley alongside our other "local" writers, and especially to compare their treatment of social class. Dickens was a famous champion of the poor, or the "deserving poor" at any rate. Gray's Elegy is laced with tributes to the "rude forefathers of the hamlet". Milton was a republican and a harsh critic of the monarchy. King claims to speak for the disorganised underclass.

But Huxley seems wholly unconcerned by the plight of his lower classes, the Deltas and Epsilons, who are chemically stunted while foetuses and then condemned to a life of menial work. It's the other end of the social scale that interests him, the Alphas and the Betas, who live comfortably but who are denied freedom, choice and risk.

54

Section 5 Slough Crematorium to Gray's Monument

Distance: 2km   Time: 30 minutes

About 300m from the crematorium gate, cross back over Stoke Road and go into the entrance to a golf driving range. Continue straight ahead past bollards blocking a lane and in 100m come to a second set of bollards. Here turn right (through a kissing-gate) and follow a public footpath across a golf course. You will be on the golf course for less than 10 minutes. Signs point the way for you, but the path is not at all evident on the ground. It crosses two fairways, so you need to be careful. Then you go into woods and come to Fir Tree Avenue, which is busy with cars.

Your next path is straight across the road. It is narrow and not well kept, but fortunately it is only 300m long. At the end of it you reach Church Lane. The monument to Thomas Gray is across the road, behind trees. (There is a gate.)

From the monument you can link to a "Heritage Walk" that takes you to St Giles churchyard, a leafy and attractive place. A tablet on the church wall shows you where Thomas Gray is buried. His own path to glory ended on 30 July 1771, following "an attack of gout in the stomach". He was just 54 years old.

Section 6 Gray's Monument to Wexham Park Hospital

Distance: 2km   Time: 30 minutes

Cross back over Church Lane from Gray's Monument. In the bushes a public footpath sign now directs you leftward through an old kissing-gate. Go along a short and rather overgrown path in front of four houses, in places coming very close to them. Just after the fourth house, go through another kissing-gate near a big red-brick house called Barton Spinney. From here your route is obvious, on a footpath alongside Barton Spinney. In 50m it takes you through another kissing-gate to the gravel street called Duffield Park. Go along it to the end, reach Gray's Park Road and cross it carefully. Turn right.

Now you have a choice.

If you don't mind loose horses and muddy fields, immediately turn left on to a tarmac road signed for Snitterfield House. A public footpath goes along this road for about 150m and then, by the gates of Snitterfield House, you should take the path that goes to your right, over a stile. Soon comes another stile and a footbridge over a ditch.

Then you go along the side of a large grassy field and through a kissing-gate at its corner. Next you go through a smaller grassy field, in which there may be many loose horses, before crossing a final stile and arriving on Wexham Street, just across from the main entrance to Wexham Park Hospital

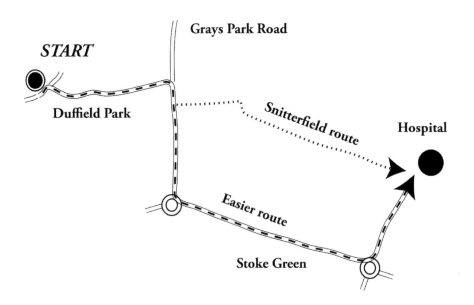

St Giles church

Alternatively, and much less challengingly, continue down Gray's Park Road to the roundabout with Stoke Green, about 250m away. Turn left along Stoke Green and in five minutes turn left up Wexham Street. Wexham Park Hospital's main gate is a couple of minutes' walk away.

By now you'll inevitably feel downcast after all these graveyards, all this talk of death. Resist the temptation to ask for *soma* at the hospital pharmacy. Just take the bus back to Slough. Spend some time with your family.

WALK 6

The Herschel Trail

The astronomer William Herschel is without doubt Slough's most renowned former resident. Working alongside his younger sister Caroline, in an observatory at their house on Windsor Road, he turned the small and unremarkable village of Slough into a place of pilgrimage for scientists, intellectuals and aristocrats. One famous astronomer said the Herschel observatory was "the place in the world where the most discoveries have been made'.

This walk honours both brother and sister by linking some of the sites associated with them, in Slough and in Datchet where they also lived for some time.

Distance: 11km.   *Time:* 2.75 hours.

Start/finish point: Slough bus station.

Transport to/from start: A bus would be the obvious choice. But Slough train station is right next door to the bus station.

Facilities on the way: Apart from the facilities in Slough town centre, there is a pub at the Red Cow roundabout and in Datchet there are pubs and shops.

Surfaces: In Slough the route follows pavements and tarmac paths, with a grit section in Herschel Park. The Datchet loop is mainly on gravel and earth paths.

Can I shorten it? You can do just the Slough part, and miss out the Datchet loop — or vice-versa. And if you want to shorten the Datchet loop you can return to Slough on the No 60 bus. (Unless you are extraordinarily gregarious it is intelligent to avoid the school bus, at about 15.15.)

Any unpleasant sections? The first part is in central Slough, which is not notably scenic, but as far as possible we go through parks and churchyards and avoid roads. The Datchet loop takes us through a golf course, albeit on a public footpath.

A NOTE ABOUT THE HERSCHELS

"The father of modern astronomy" is a common tag for William Herschel. He became *Sir* William in 1816, the knighthood honouring a long and distinguished career. Born in Germany in 1738 he moved to England in 1757 and worked as a musician before taking up astronomy. In 1781 his discovery of the planet Uranus brought him immediate fame. He was elected as a Fellow of the Royal Society and appointed as the "king's astronomer" — and it was the royal appointment that brought him to the Slough area, to be near to his patron, King George III.

He made many more discoveries, notably about the moons of Uranus and Saturn and about the planet Mars. Conducting experiments on light and heat, he identified the electromagnetic radiation we now call "infra-red". His theoretical work helped shape the modern way of seeing the universe, as a shifting collection of planetary bodies in expanding space rather than as a kind of clockwork apparatus that does not change.

Many discoveries were made possible by the sometimes heroic efforts of Herschel's sister Caroline, first as his assistant and then as a more equal partner. In 1828 the Royal Astronomical Society acknowledged her contribution by awarding her its Gold Medal, and in 1835 she was elected as an honorary member.

Slough bus station

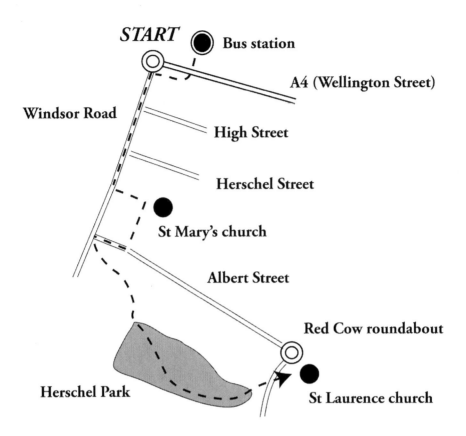

START

Bus station

A4 (Wellington Street)

Windsor Road

High Street

Herschel Street

St Mary's church

Albert Street

Red Cow roundabout

Herschel Park

St Laurence church

Section 1 *Slough Bus Station to Red Cow Roundabout*

Distance: 2km   Time: 30 minutes

Start at Slough bus station, whose distinctive wavy roof was inspired by Herschel's infra-red experiments. It's worth taking a moment to study the structure, even though your behaviour may be considered eccentric by passers-by. Not everyone appreciates the bold new design. "It looks like a beached whale which has had all of its back-end eaten away by scavengers," one passenger told a BBC reporter.

When you are ready to move on, go up to the A4 (Wellington Street), cross it and turn right, then turn left down Windsor Road. Cross High Street and continue down to Herschel Street.

Observatory House, where William Herschel lived for 36 years, stood on the site of the office block now occupied by Fujitsu. The old house, sadly, was demolished in the early 1960s.

When William and Caroline moved here in 1786, they had all the trees cut down so they could better "sweep" the night sky with their telescopes. The biggest of the telescopes, 40 feet long, became a famous landmark and was shown on Ordnance Survey maps.

A sculpture in memory of William is situated near the corner of Herschel Street and Windsor Road. An abstract piece by Czech artist Franta Belsky, it has an inscription saying it "symbolises the triangular structure of the forty foot telescope through which [Herschel] reached up to encompass the infinite".

Continue down Windsor Road for about 150m, turn left through an iron gate and follow a tarmac path through St Mary's churchyard. At the church itself, go right, down a tarmac drive. At the end of it turn right, along Albert Street. At the traffic lights go left down Windsor Road then immediately go left, through gates, on a tarmac road. In 150m turn right, down another tarmac road and in less than 100m enter Herschel Park through gates on your left.

The park has been nicely restored recently and is worth exploring. But for now take the right-hand grit track and follow it down to the bridge between the two ponds. Don't cross the bridge, but turn left on another grit track. Keep right at the next two track junctions and go into the "Herschel Park Nature Reserve". Turn left on the low-level track and come in about 300m to Datchet Road.

Herschel sculpture

Section 2   Red Cow Roundabout to Datchet Golf Course

Distance: 1.5km   Time: 20 minutes

Turn right, along Datchet Road. In about 250m, immediately after crossing the M4 motorway, turn right again, on to a footpath. Follow it down a ramp to the Myrke and then go alongside this row of Victorian houses.

After the Myrke road bends to the left, continue along it for another 150m. Then, when you are opposite the last of the houses, turn right through a swing gate on to a grit track signed "Jubilee Bridleway". It follows the course of the Jubilee River (which is hidden behind a flood-defence rampart on your right) and takes you in about five minutes to Pococks Lane (which you reach through another swing gate).

Cross Pococks Lane very carefully, for the traffic hurries around the bend, and go along a gravel footpath that starts a few paces to your right. Soon, after passing a water pumping station, it brings you close to the Jubilee River and takes you through an arch in a rail bridge.

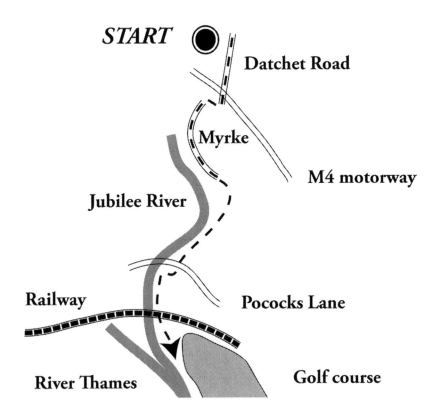

Looking back to the railway bridge. Here the Jubilee River flows into the Thames.

Section 3   Datchet Golf Course to Datchet village

Distance: 2km   Time: 30 minutes

Soon after the rail bridge your path goes into Datchet golf course. A warning sign tells you to keep to the path and look out for flying golf balls. The path is grassy to begin with, then gravel. In about 15 minutes it brings you to Windsor Road, on the edge of Datchet.

Turn left and then in 150m go left again, along Queen Street, and come to the village centre. About 200m to your right, near a roundabout and beside a tall-steepled church, is the Royal Stag pub.

The Herschels moved to Datchet in 1782. They came by coach to Slough, then walked the rest of the way and lodged a night in the Royal Stag, called in those days the Five Bells Inn. One of the oldest buildings in the village, it is an atmospheric place with a room full of stag heads. And it has the obligatory spookish presence, which leaves a ghostly hand-print on a window pane. (If you tell the bar staff you can't see it they'll suggest you need another drink.)

After their night at the Five Bells, William and Caroline made the short walk to their new lodgings, a house called The Lawns that was located about 500m to the southeast of the inn, and just to the north of the Horton Road.

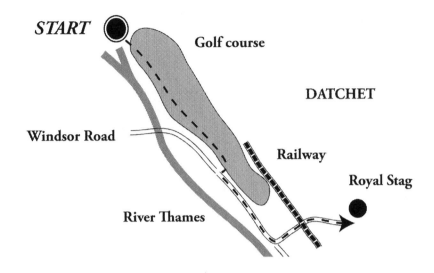

START

Golf course

DATCHET

Windsor Road

Railway

Royal Stag

River Thames

Caroline, who had not previously seen the house, was appalled. She described it as "the ruins of a place which had once served as a hunting seat to some Gentleman and had not been inhabited for years". The roof leaked and the garden was a wilderness — and the servant who should have greeted them was in prison for theft.

(Caroline was rather outspoken and present-day Slough residents might enjoy her rant about the perfidy of Datchet traders: everything was too expensive; the butcher over-charged and "would not give honest weight". Datchet residents might equally enjoy her complaints about the 'swarm of pilfering work-people, with which Slough … was particularly infested'.)

The house turned out to be uncomfortably close to the flood-prone Thames. This made the business of observing the night sky, from a telescope in the backyard, especially onerous for William, who 'when the waters were out round his garden, used to rub himself all over, face and hands &c., with a raw onion, to keep off the infection of the ague, which was then prevalent.'

After three winters, both brother and sister had had enough, and in search of a drier place they moved first to Old Windsor — where they stayed for only nine months, then left following a dispute with their landlady — and subsequently to Slough. Unsurprisingly, their Datchet house no longer survives.

(Section 4 Retrace your steps to Red Cow roundabout)
(Distance: 3.5km   Time: 50 minutes)

Section 5   Red Cow Roundabout to Slough Bus Station

Distance: 2km   Time: 30 minutes

At the Red Cow roundabout turn right, into Upton Court Road, and immediately go into the churchyard of St Laurence. William Herschel is buried under the tower and is commemorated by the church's Herschel Windows, which depict the solar system. They are best seen from inside the building, so this route is nice on one of St Laurence's open days, when the verger leads a quirky tour and you can buy a lifetime supply of jam.

When you leave the churchyard, cross Upton Court Road, go right and then immediately left into Upton Road. Halfway along, at number 74, is a distinctive black and white house. It once belonged to Mary Pitt, whom William Herschel married in 1788.

Out of consideration for Caroline, the newlyweds for a time ran two households — at Upton Road and at Windsor Road. Initially Caroline continued to live at the Windsor Road property, but she moved to Upton Road in 1803 and lived there until 1810. (It seems she was unhappy with the domestic changes brought about by the marriage, particularly her loss of status and responsibility.)

The Upton Road house

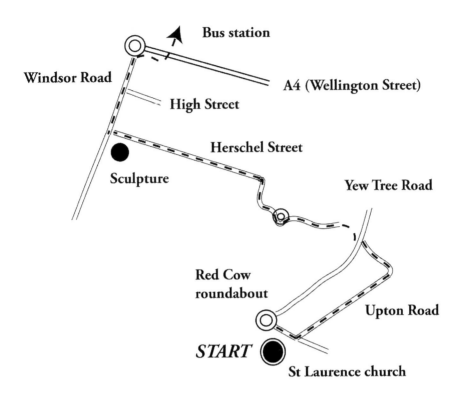

Continue to the end of Upton Road and cross Yew Tree Road. Turn right and in a few paces go left along an alley to Merton Road. Keeping to the left footway, follow Merton Road to a roundabout and go straight ahead, along Alpha Street North. In 50m it bends to the right and in a further 100m you turn left into Herschel Street.

On the way along Herschel Street you pass the back of the BHS store. It is on, or near, a site once occupied by "Elizabeth Cottage" where Caroline Herschel lodged for a time. As we saw in Walk 5, the cottage also has associations with Charles Dickens.

On the five-minute walk to the far end of Herschel Street you'll come near to Herschel Medical Centre, go past the Herschel Arms pub and the Herschel Multi-storey Car Park, and then come again to the Herschel Sculpture, from where you can make your way back to the bus station.

WALK 7

A Short Walk to Mesopotamia

This walk follows an off-the-beaten-track route through the bordering communities of Slough town and Eton College. They haven't always been the chummiest of neighbours. In the 1830s the College opposed the building of a station for Slough on the London railway line. In the 1840s it opposed the Slough to Windsor line altogether. In the 1870s Slough's arm of the Grand Union Canal had to be re-planned in the face of College resistance. In the 1890s the College bought land in north Eton mainly to block Slough's southward expansion and in the 1920s it extended the *cordon sanitaire* by purchasing more land near Cippenham and Chalvey.

In modern times the M4 motorway and the Jubilee River have combined symbolically as a moated rampart, cutting off even visual contact. But recently there have been small signs of *rapprochement* and in 2008 the College signed up to an Independent and State School Partnership that has opened some of its facilities to kids from Slough. Admittedly it reserves for itself a *noblesse oblige* sort of lead-role in the partnership, but maybe it's a start.

Distance: 8km. *Time:* 2 hours.

Start/finish point: Slough's former Town Hall on Bath Road.

Transport to/from start: Number 75/76 buses stop near the old Town Hall.

Facilities on the way: Both Chalvey and Eton have shops and pubs.

Surfaces: In Chalvey and parts of Eton you are mainly on tarmac. Other parts of Eton have grit tracks, as does the Jubilee River section — which has several kissing-gates.

Can I shorten it? You could split it into two outings. One would be from the former Town Hall to the Jubilee River and back. The other would be the Eton loop, which you could do from the Jubilee River car park on Windsor Road, just south of the M4 motorway.

Any unpleasant sections? The section between Chalvey and the Jubilee River involves a combination of features that would disbar it from many walkers' guidebooks: a sex-trade district, a refuse disposal plant and a motorway.

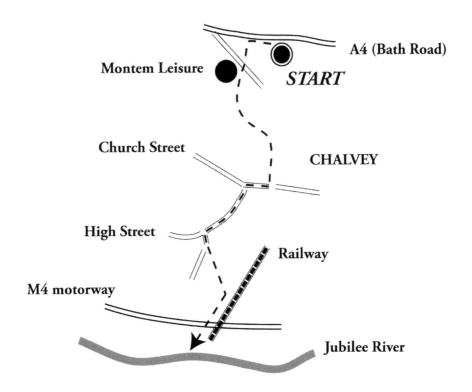

A4 (Bath Road)

Montem Leisure

START

Church Street

CHALVEY

High Street

Railway

M4 motorway

Jubilee River

Section 1   *Former Town Hall to Jubilee River*

Distance: 1.5km   Time: 25 minutes

From the old Town Hall walk west along Bath Road for 150m then turn left down a short public footpath. Go straight across Montem Lane and down the tarmac footpath to Montem Leisure Centre's main car park, then turn *sharp* left on to the grass of Montem Recreation Ground. About 50m away there is a gap in the metal fence. Go through it and turn right, along an alley. In just over 100m go right, down another alley and in 150m come to Chalvey Road.

A wall beside the second alley carries a spray-painted admonition about the lure of sin. *Shatan came to Adam and Eve and said 'You are in Paradise but you are not free to do everything. Don't make any boundary or limitation for yourself.'* But it is clear that not everyone can resist Shatan's tempting. Just five minutes away is a favoured haunt of street prostitutes, and the police do periodic culls of kerb-crawlers, netting dozens each time. In court one defendant submitted that although the "voice of the Lord" had advised him to seek a massage, the "voice of the devil" had urged him to ask instead for sex. The magistrate, having none of it, fined him £400 plus £95 costs.

Jubilee River (near TVAC)

Cross Chalvey Road, turn right and almost immediately turn left down High Street. Soon turn left into Spackmans Way and after crossing Primary Road go left along a tarmac bridleway signposted for the Jubilee River. In about 200m, beside a recycling centre and just before a railway line, turn right at a Y-junction. Now follow another tarmac path under the M4 motorway and, with the railway immediately to your left, soon cross a bridge over the Jubilee River.

Even a short stroll through Chalvey will show you that it has prosperous areas. And some of the Victorian streets, in particular, are models of solid respectability. But there are obvious pockets of poverty. If you want the statistics, look at Slough Borough Council's 2010 report on The Index of Multiple Deprivation. Slough is among the 30% most deprived local authorities in England and some of its most deprived neighbourhoods are in Chalvey.

Eton boating (on the Thames)

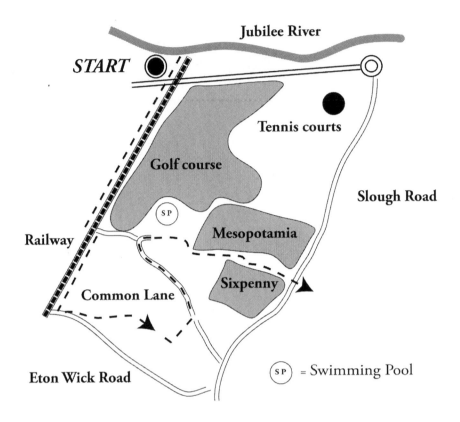

Section 2 Jubilee River to Mesopotamia

Distance: 2.5km   Time: 35 minutes

After the bridge continue straight ahead, on a tarmac track, and follow the railway line south toward Windsor. The College opposed the construction of the railway on the grounds that the students would find it distracting. And that was prophetic, for when it did come the boys stoned the carriages, even on one occasion when they contained royal passengers. Some boys, in a later century, would themselves get stoned in the railway arches, a misdemeanour that lost them privileges but did not prevent them holding high office in adult life.

After almost one kilometre your tarmac track turns left and goes under the railway line. Follow it under, then immediately turn right on to a grit track alongside the railway arches. In 250m it brings you to Eton Wick Road. Go left for about 50m, then turn obliquely left on an earth path through a grassy field. In just over 100m pass through a staggered gate and join a slab path down a narrow alley.

To your left, behind a high fence, is one of 25 Houses that provide accommodation for the 1300 students. It's a higher concentration of public schoolboys than you'd find even in the House of Commons, and if you come in mid-morning when the students move back to their Houses for "Chambers" (elevenses) you need to be ready for a backwards-in-time sort of experience.

Hundreds of the teenagers mill around, wearing regulation School Dress tailcoat and pin-stripes. Quaint notices on House gates direct them to the Boys' Entrance, away from the offices of Housemaster and Dame and most decidedly away from the Tradesman's Entrance. The tradesmen themselves go past on upright black bicycles mounted with the kind of baggage-carriers that were cutting-edge a century ago.

You'll also see gowned teachers — lots of them, for there are 160 full-timers on site, assisted by almost 100 part-time and sessional staff. This produces a pupil-teacher ratio that the state sector can only dream about. The teachers style themselves as Masters, but the students call them "beaks".

"With its own language and traditions, not least the distinctive uniform", says the College prospectus, "Eton creates a world in which boys are recognised for their character and their achievement, not their background". That's a lovely thought, but whether you will find it convincing may depend on your reaction to these numbers: the yearly fee at Eton is almost £36,000 and most boys stay five years; the average annual salary of Slough residents is about £27,000.

Looking back along the rail-side path

When you come to a T-junction go left, and then in 20m go right, alongside Holland House. Your alleyway is now called Judy's Passage, an evident source of local mirth and a popular topic in pub quizzes: *In which English town can you see a beak go up Judy's Passage?*

The passage ends at Common Lane, very close to the High Street and within sight of the iconic College Chapel. Turn left along Common Lane and in 50m look up at the curious horizontal statue that juts from the third storey of Common Lane House. Called *Edge II*, it is the work of sculptor Antony Gormley, whose website explains that it is part of a series that "attempts to destabilise the normal projected subjective coordinates of front/back, left/right, up/down."

You'll no doubt want to mull that over, but for now continue along Common Lane until you are almost back at the railway line. However, just before the College golf course and the College astronomical observatory, turn right on a tarmac drive, following a sign to Swimming Pool Cottages.

Go past the cottages and the large cylindrical tanks of the outdoor pool, then go through a gate and on to a gravel track. This will take you alongside a stream that the Ordnance Survey map calls Colenorton Brook but which is "Jordan" in Eton-speak. The adjacent cricket field is "Mesopotamia".

Soon you reach a brick bridge on your right. Cross it and come to Sixpenny Field. Now turn left and follow a wide gravel track through the middle arch of a bridge that carries the Slough Road.

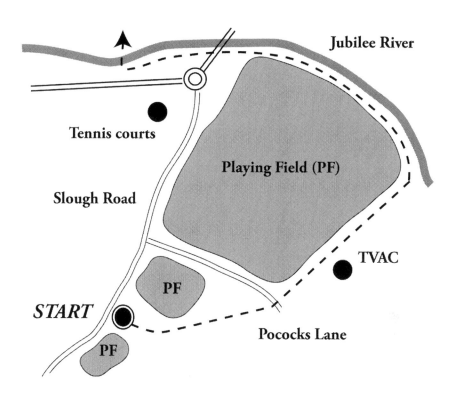

Section 3   Mesopotamia to Jubilee River-crossing

Distance: 2km   Time: 30 minutes

About 100m after the road bridge, turn left and cross a footbridge beside a pond (Fellow's Pond). Then immediately turn obliquely right, on to a footpath that runs roughly parallel to the River Thames and brings you in 250m to Pocock's Lane.

Carefully cross the road and join a grit track that will take you alongside manicured playing fields (Agar's Plough and Dutchman's Field) to the Jubilee River. To your right is Thames Valley Athletics Centre (TVAC).

Usually the playing fields host rugby and cricket matches, but a sign erected by the Provost and Fellows of Eton College warns that a "beagle pack has authorised use of these grounds". If you come on the Fourth of June open day you'll not only see the dogs in action but you can also watch a game of polo in full cry, the boys thundering up and down Dutchman's Field, changing ponies at the end of each chukka. It's all vital preparation for the time when schooldays must end and merging into the wider community is called for.

On reaching the Jubilee River turn left, and follow a bridleway along the south bank. In about 10 minutes cross Windsor Road at a controlled crossing and continue along the river bank. On your left, on the other side of the Relief Road spur, are some of the College's 29 tennis courts.

At the next footbridge, soon after a weir, go across the river.

Montem Mound

Section 4   *Jubilee River-crossing to former Town Hall*
Distance: 2km   Time: 30 minutes

Once across the river, turn left along a bridleway that soon goes through a kissing-gate then bears right, under the motorway. Just beyond the motorway, turn left under the railway line, then turn right at the Y-junction you passed in Section 1.

When you reach a road, veer right, along the tarmac alley you used earlier. Follow it to Spackmans Way and soon turn right, on to High Street. In 50m cross High Street and go *straight ahead*, along The Green. Soon after the Garibaldi pub turn right, into Clive Court, at the end of which is the church of St Peter. Go into the churchyard, follow a path round the church and then cross Church Street. Turn right, then go immediately left along Newbery Way.

In less than 100m go through a staggered gate into Montem Recreation Ground and immediately turn left on an earth path. Follow it alongside Chalvey Brook for about 500m until you come to the A4 (Bath Road). Here you can turn right and make your way back to the former town hall.

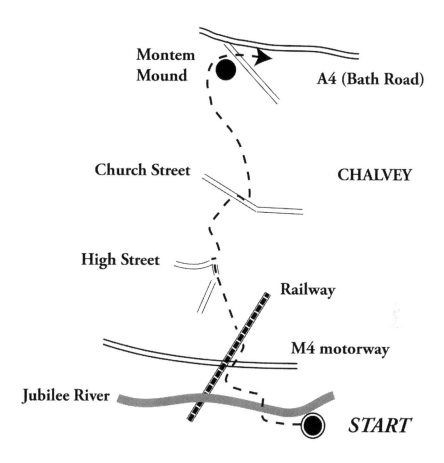

Montem Mound

A4 (Bath Road)

Church Street

CHALVEY

High Street

Railway

M4 motorway

Jubilee River

START

But first you should make a detour to the grassy Montem Mound, just 50m away. Opinion is divided as to whether it is a Bronze Age burial site or a Norman *motte*. What is certain is that it was used for centuries by Eton boys, in a ceremony in which charitable donations were demanded from passers-by in a menacing way, an early form of chugging.

An account written in 1560 describes the mound as "a sacred spot in the boyish religion of Etonians ... on account of the beauty of the country, the charm of the greensward, the coolness of the shade, the tuneful chorus of the birds, they dedicate the retreat to Apollo and the Muses, they celebrate it in verses, call it Tempe and extol it above Helicon."

You'll probably notice that things have changed a bit since those days.

WALK 8

The Narrowboat Way

This route starts and finishes on the Slough Arm of the Grand Union Canal, once known locally as The Cut.

When it first opened, in 1882, the Slough Arm became part of an extensive canal network which had been expanding since the start of the nineteenth century and which already extended from London to Birmingham. The Slough section was built mainly to serve the town's growing brick-making industry, and for a time it experienced good levels of traffic.

However, in about 1905 a decline set in — and then progressively gathered pace — the result of decreasing mineral reserves and increasing competition from the railways. The last commercial traffic was carried in 1960. The town council then proposed to build a road along the canal route, or at least part of it, but a vigorous local campaign halted the plan and the waterway was reopened as a leisure facility in 1975.

Distance: 10.5km.   *Time:* 2.5 hours.

Start/finish point: Langley station.

Transport to/from start: Train to Langley station or choice of buses between Slough bus station and Langley Harrow shopping centre, a few minutes' walk from Langley station.

Facilities on the way: There is a wide range of shops at Langley Harrow. A short detour in Iver brings you to shops and pubs. In Langley Park you can detour to a café.

Surfaces: The canal towpath is a mix of grit track and earth path. Elsewhere you are mainly on earth paths. There are kissing-gates on the canal towpath, at the south side of Iver and in Langley Park.

Can I shorten it? From Iver you can take a No 58 bus through Langley to Slough bus station.

Any unpleasant sections? The Bellswood Lane section, near Langley Park, involves road walking and there is no footway.

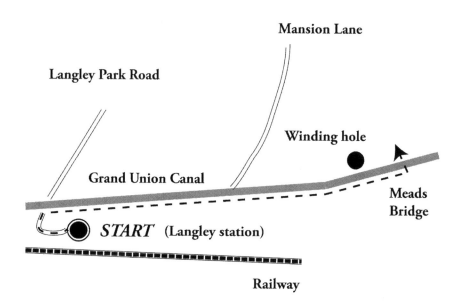

Mansion Lane

Langley Park Road

Winding hole

Grand Union Canal

Meads Bridge

START (Langley station)

Railway

Section 1   Langley Station to Meads Bridge

Distance: 2km   Time: 30 minutes

Go out of the station car park and turn right, along Langley Park Road. In about 100m reach the canal at a humpback bridge and, without crossing the bridge, turn right on a footpath that will take you down to the towpath. Walk east, so that the water is on your left. Moored on the opposite bank there will be a long line of narrowboats, usually stretching all the way to Mansion Lane, a distance of almost one kilometre.

Faced with these gaily-coloured vessels it is easy to get starry-eyed about canal-life and you might want to learn more about it. If so you should visit Slough Canal Festival, which is held in Bloom Park every September. During the two-day event you can take a boat-trip along to the Slough basin, buy boat-ware painted in the traditional *roses and castles* style, and even experience other vestigial bucolic stuff like falconry and ferret-racing. Sometimes, as the Slough Express has reported, "Farmer Thomas Longton from Lancashire brings along his award-winning sheepdogs Maya and Tot, for a display of geese and duck shepherding".

If, after seeing all that, you're ready to quit town-life and go vagabonding round Britain's waterways, the Mansion Lane boatyard can sell you a vessel. Fifty thousand pounds will get you a brand new fifty-footer.

Near Langley station, looking east

You will also need a little help with the colourful terminology that canal boating has accumulated. Some of it can be scary. One boaters' video advises, "You *can* steer a butty with the ellum not in its pintles. But it's guinea a minute." A good place to start is the website run by enthusiast Tony Ward (see *References and Reading*). It contains a wide collection of boatmen's words and phrases ("about 648 of them at the last count"). If you want to know how to tell a noggin from a false cratch, or a gongoozler from a gonguzzler, it's the place to go.

But be warned: the reality of narrowboating may not quite match the romantic image. Even with modern conveniences it can be cold and dark. (The picture above was taken in late March, but there is still ice on the water.) And if you look back in time the romantic image can seem altogether fanciful.

The Slough Arm was opened in 1882, soon after the passing of the Canal Boats Act. The legislation owed much to the efforts of a social reformer called George Smith who in 1875 had written a book called Our Canal Population. The book highlighted the appalling conditions suffered by many canal families, for whom their boat's tiny aft cabin was their year-round home.

"Some of the canal cabins are models of neatness," Smith wrote, "and a man and two youths might pass a few nights in such very comfortably. Others are the most filthy holes imaginable, what with bugs and other vermin creeping up the sides, stinking mud finding its way through the leaky joints ... and being heated by a hot stove, stenches arise therefrom to make a dog sick. In these cabins fathers, mothers, sisters and brothers sleep in the same bed at the same time. In these places girls of 17 give birth to children, fathers of which are members of their own family."

Matters were made worse by the often foul condition of the waterways themselves. Human excrement would be tipped over the sides of the boats, but then canal water would be used for washing and drinking. On the Slough Arm, public health was further endangered by the cargoes transported: on their way back from London the boats often carried household rubbish and horse manure.

To continue your walk, proceed along the canal towpath, now making your way toward Iver. This section is quite rural in nature and is generally attractive. You will leave the waterway at Meads Bridge, about 1km beyond Mansion Lane. About 150m before you reach Meads Bridge look out for an inlet on the opposite bank. This is Meads Bridge Winding Hole, a place where boatmen could turn their vessels through 180 degrees. Nearby were wharves where the London-bound boats would be loaded with newly-made bricks.

At Mansion Lane

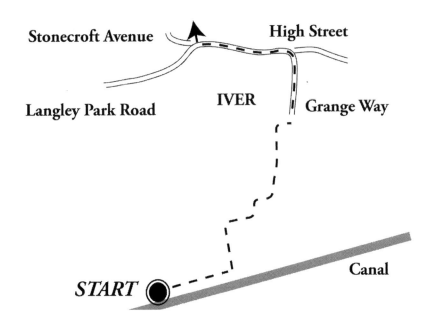

Stonecroft Avenue

High Street

Langley Park Road

IVER

Grange Way

Canal

START

Section 2 Meads Bridge to Iver High Street

Distance: 2km Time: 30 minutes

Iver was at the east end of the Slough and Langley brickfields, which covered a vast area that produced millions of bricks a year. One brickfield lay between the canal and the village itself, to which you are now headed.

Go over Meads Bridge and in 50m turn right, along a grassy path below power cables. After a few minutes the path will take you round the boundary of Ridgeway industrial estate. Then you turn left and follow the path up to Iver. At the edge of a housing estate turn right then immediately go left along Grange Way to reach High Street. Go left along High Street for five minutes, until you reach an obvious bend. Here, beside Stonecroft Avenue, you go to the right, along a public footpath.

Like canal-boating, brickmaking relied heavily on child labour. And like canal-boating it attracted the reforming zeal of George Smith. Born in Staffordshire in 1831, Smith had been sent to work in a brickyard at the age of seven, carrying clay to the drying floors and bricks from the kilns. By the time he was nine he regularly worked a thirteen-hour day. As an adult he campaigned to have the Factory Act extended to brickyards, finally succeeding in 1871. But the effect was only partial. Even in the 1890s teachers at Iver Girls' School reported that pupils frequently missed school and went instead to the brickfields.

Section 3   Iver High Street to Langley Park Lake

Distance: 3km   Time: 45 minutes

At the bend on Iver High Street turn right, on to the footpath. In less than five minutes it will take you to Love Green. Go left along Love Green Road and in 50m go across the tiny green on the other side of the road. Then cross Swallow Street, go right for just over 50m then turn left, along a bridleway signed as Cycleway Route 61.

It soon passes between grassy fields and in about 10 minutes brings you to Wood Lane.

Go straight across Wood Lane and continue down Bellswood Lane (taking especial care, as there is no footway). Then cross Billet Lane and go down a tarmac drive past Treal Farm and into Langley Park.

Here, if you like, you can detour to the visitors' centre and café, a few minutes to your right. Otherwise go straight ahead on a grit track for almost 10 minutes, passing an arboretum and then a large red-brick building, and come to a crossroads beside the gates of Langley Park House.

Here go obliquely to the right, along a broad grit road, and in about 300m turn left through a kissing gate to arrive at Langley Park Lake.

Once a royal deer park, Langley Park estate became in 1738 the property of Charles Spencer, third Duke of Marlborough.

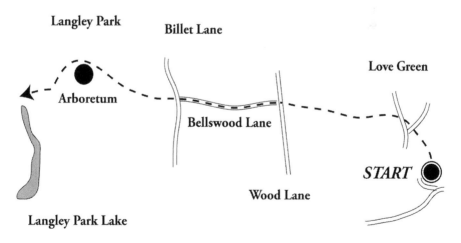

The arboretum at Langley Park

Already the owner of Blenheim Palace, a colossally extravagant "pile of stones" with nearly 200 rooms, Spencer was hardly short of space. Yet among his early improvements at Langley was the construction of a "banqueting pavilion". Next came a mansion, to replace the existing house.

Then, in 1763, carrying on his dad's good work, the *fourth* Duke commissioned Lancelot "Capability" Brown to landscape the park. One of the features needing attention was a large rectangular pond, which had once been the clay pit that had produced the bricks for the old house.

Brown charged a fee of £2810 for the design work, his plan including the reshaped serpentine lake that we see today. (To put that in perspective: in the Iver brickfields, even 150 years later "the pay for a fourteen-year-old girl was 9s a week for working twelve hours a day." (Rowlands, 2003.) Nine shillings a week amounted to less than £25 a year.)

In 1788 the Spencers sold up to the Harvey family, who demolished the banqueting pavilion and replaced it in 1865 with the Harvey Memorial Tower, a lighthouse-like structure with a viewing platform reached up a stairway of 100 steps. Its sole purpose was to afford fine views of Windsor Castle.

One hopes that the arboretum was by then doing its job, and shielded the genteel viewers from any disagreeable sightings of ragged kids working on brickfield or canal.

Section 4   Langley Park Lake to Langley station

Distance: 3.5km   Time: 50 minutes

Follow a path alongside the lake, and at the end of the water continue ahead for 50m until you can turn left on an earth footpath. Follow it for 200m, crossing a stream by a wooden footbridge, and then turn right through a gate. You are now on a path that will take you in 10 minutes to Orchards Residential Park. When you reach it go straight ahead, first along a short road and then along a shorter alleyway that takes you to a footbridge over a stream. There you join an earth path that leads in a few minutes to a pedestrian bridge over the canal. Cross it and go down to the towpath. Then turn east, so that the water is on your left, and walk along to the bridge at Langley Park Road. Turn right and return to Langley station.

There were once brickfields on both sides of the canal here, and others as far west as central Slough. When the clay was exhausted, the pits and other excavations were filled with household refuse, the detritus of a million London homes, brought by hundreds of barges making thousands of journeys.

Keep that in mind the next time your kids complain that *Slough is rubbish*. They're not wrong.

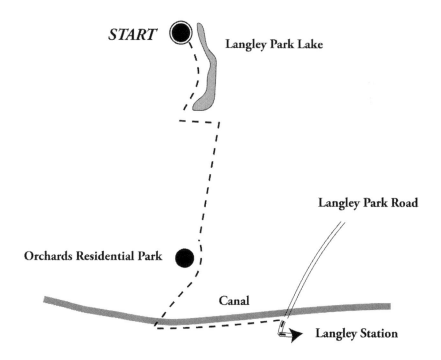

WALK 9

The Inner Circle

This walk aims to provide a satisfying circuit that stays wholly inside the Borough boundary. And it almost succeeds. Mainly following footpaths and bridleways, it links parks and open spaces and includes two nature reserves. On the way it passes two historic sites. The idea is to offer a "Slough in a Nutshell" sort of itinerary, for times when you want to get to know the town better — or just to stretch your legs.

One part of the route also features in Walks 1 and 3. Some of it also features in Walk 10.

The route directions are necessarily quite long and detailed. Therefore, to keep the chapter to a manageable length, very little "sightseeing" information has been included.

Distance: 14.5km.   *Time:* 3.75 hours.

Start/finish point: It is a circular route, so you can begin wherever you like. The description given here starts at the former Town Hall.

Facilities on the way: There is a cafe in Salt Hill Park. There are pubs at Farnham Royal and Lynch Hill. The Asda supermarket in Cippenham has a fast-food café.

Surfaces: Much of the route is on tarmac but there are earth paths between Cocksherd Wood and Burnham station. The Jubilee River track is gravel.

Can I shorten it? Yes. The easiest way would be to split it into sections to the north and south of the A4 road respectively.

Any unpleasant sections? The Cinder Track has a bad reputation. One website for young people says "Walk down their if you have a death wish and wish to have your stomach ripped out and found again on the oppsite end" (sic). Nevertheless it is well used — by a mix of families, single walkers and cyclists. During the school run it is especially busy, particularly at the southern end. But it does get lonelier as you go north.

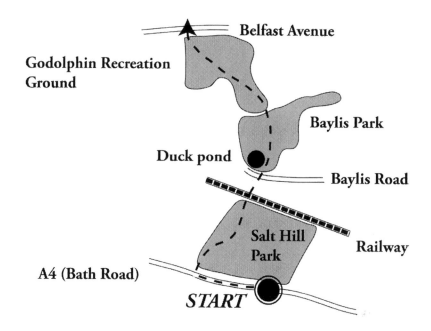

Belfast Avenue

Godolphin Recreation
Ground

Baylis Park

Duck pond

Baylis Road

Salt Hill
Park

Railway

A4 (Bath Road)

START

Section 1   Former Town Hall to Cinder Track

Distance: 2km   Time: 30 minutes

From the old Town Hall go west along the A4 (Bath Road) for 200m, cross Montem Lane and then in under 100m cross the A4 at a controlled crossing. Go right for 50m then turn left into Salt Hill Park.

Keep straight ahead on a tarmac track, soon with a stream on your left. In a few minutes the stream goes into a culvert and your track bears a little to the left before going under the railway. It then bends to the right. Almost immediately you should turn left on another track and go up to Baylis Road.

Cross Baylis Road and go into Baylis Park. Pass to the right of the duck pond, keep straight ahead, and in about 50m come to a path junction. Go straight ahead, so that you soon have the red brick walls and white iron fences of Baylis House on your right. Just beyond Baylis House you cross a stream and come into Godolphin Recreation Ground. Here the track divides into four.

Go straight ahead, on the most dominant track. In five minutes it will take you to the far corner of the recreation ground and on the way you will go straight ahead at a staggered junction. At the corner you leave the park along an alley that soon comes to Belfast Avenue. Go straight across, to join the Cinder Track.

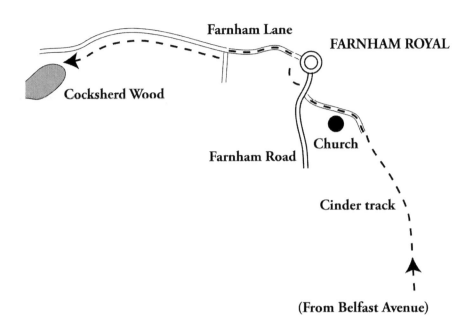

Farnham Lane

FARNHAM ROYAL

Cocksherd Wood

Church

Farnham Road

Cinder track

(From Belfast Avenue)

Section 2   Cinder Track to Cocksherd Wood

Distance: 3km   Time: 45 minutes

You will stay on the Cinder Track for about 20 minutes, making several more road-crossings. Despite the name, the surface is tarmac all the way. Initially quite urban in character, the track gets leafier — and much less well-trodden — as you go north. At the end of it you join Church Road, which you then follow along to Farnham Road.

Turn right into Farnham Road, immediately cross it at a controlled crossing and go straight on down a short tarmac lane between modern brick houses.

At the end of the lane turn right and make the short walk over to Farnham Lane. Turn left and follow Farnham Lane for about 15 minutes. This section involves road-side walking but it becomes more pleasant in a few minutes when there are lawns between you and the main road.

When the lawns end your progress seems barred by a metal fence with high trees beyond it. But this is Cocksherd Wood, sometimes known locally as Bluebell Wood. It is a nature reserve, and there is a swing gate, which you should now go through.

Section 3   Cocksherd Wood to Burnham Station

Distance: 2km   Time: 30 minutes

Go straight ahead on a broad earth path that first runs roughly parallel to the road but then bends to the left and goes down a flight of steps. Soon it comes to a Y-junction at which you should go left. After 50m go straight ahead, at first alongside a metal fence, then continue forward to Lynch Hill Lane.

Cross over and go into Lynch Hill Park, a broad expanse of grass. Follow an earth path straight ahead for 10 minutes, then climb a flight of steps and come to Long Furlong Drive. Cross it and go into another grassy park, Lammas Meadow. Now follow an earth path for about three minutes and come to Whittaker Road. Across Whittaker Road is Haymill Valley Nature Reserve, known locally as "The Millie". Near its right-hand corner is a kissing-gate. Go through it and keep straight on along an earth path. It follows a winding course, but runs more or less parallel to Littlebrook Avenue. There are several forks to the left, but ignore them.

After less than 10 minutes, when your path comes for the first time right up to the metal fence, leave The Millie and go up to Littlebrook Avenue. Turn left and in about 100m keep straight ahead to go through a short alleyway between metal fences. Then carefully cross Burnham Lane and Station Road and reach the driveway of Burnham railway station.

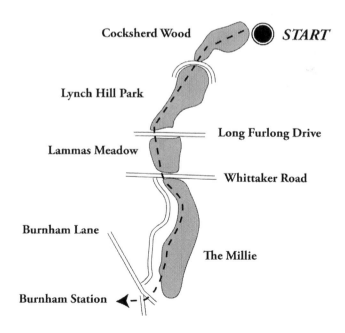

87

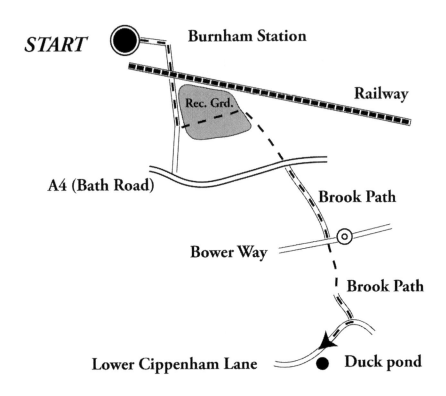

START

Burnham Station

Railway

Rec. Grd.

A4 (Bath Road)

Brook Path

Bower Way

Brook Path

Lower Cippenham Lane

Duck pond

Section 4 Burnham Station to Lower Cippenham Lane

Distance: 1.5km Time: 20 minutes

Go down Station Road and through the railway arch. Then carefully re-cross Station Road and continue alongside a hedge for a couple of minutes until you can turn left into Cippenham Recreation Ground. Go through this pleasant small park on a tarmac track and immediately beyond the far boundary turn right on another tarmac track.

At a staggered junction keep straight ahead and come in a few minutes to the busy A4 (Bath Road).

The next stage goes along Brook Path, which is directly across the A4. But to get across to it you will need to detour to your left for about 150m and cross at the traffic lights by Burnham Lane.

Brook Path has alternating sections of roadway and pathway but it is easy to follow and in about seven minutes brings you to Lower Cippenham Lane at an obvious bend in the road.

Statue on Baylis Road (Section 1 of the walk)

Cippenham Recreation Ground (Section 4)

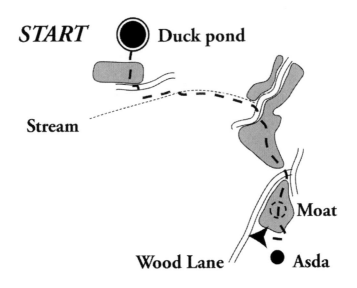

START   ● Duck pond

Stream

Moat

Wood Lane   ● Asda

(The shaded areas are green spaces)

Section 5   Lower Cippenham Lane to Asda Supermarket

Distance: 1.5km   Time: 20 minutes

Cross Lower Cippenham Lane, turn right and then in 100m turn left down a tarmac footpath beside the Village Pond. Keep straight on through the tiny Deerwood Park and come to Earls Lane. Here go left for 50m then cross the road and just after a bridge turn right, along a tarmac pathway with a stream on your right.

In 50m turn left at a path crossroads. You now have a different stream on your right. In a couple of minutes your path crosses that stream and then follows it on the other bank for a few minutes until it reaches Richards Way.

Cross Richards Way and follow a tarmac track through "Little Chapels Way Open Space". Ahead of you is the distinctive tower of the Asda supermarket.

In a couple of minutes you come to Wood Lane near its junction with Telford Drive. Cross the road, then turn left into Telford Drive and follow the pavement round for a few paces until you can go into the grassy grounds of Cippenham Moat at a staggered gate.

Go to the far end of the grassy grounds, after looking round the site. Then turn right along a tarmac path and reach Wood Lane.

Cippenham Pond

Cippenham Moat

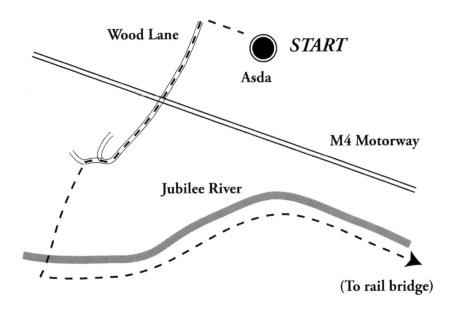

Wood Lane

START

Asda

M4 Motorway

Jubilee River

(To rail bridge)

Section 6   Asda Supermarket to former Town Hall

Distance: 4.5km   Time: 75 minutes

Turn left and follow Wood Lane across the motorway. After the motorway, Wood Lane goes downhill and bends to the right just before a line of houses. At the bend turn left, then very soon go left again — at a boom gate — and join a broad tarmac bridleway. Stay on it and go over the Jubilee River at a footbridge. Then turn left and follow the riverside bridleway until you reach a rail bridge (about 40 minutes' walk from Asda).

Cross the Jubilee River on the footbridge beside the rail bridge. Continue under the motorway, and when you reach the recycling plant follow a tarmac alley up to the junction of Spackmans Way and High Street. Turn right, into High Street, cross it and go straight on along The Green. Soon after passing the Garibaldi pub turn right into Clive Court where you will see the church of St Peter. Go down a few steps into the churchyard, follow the path past the church and come to Church Street. Cross it carefully, turn right and then go immediately left along Newbery Way, with the Chalvey Brook on your left.

In less than 100m go through a staggered gate into Montem Recreation Ground and immediately turn left on an earth path. Follow it alongside the brook for a few minutes until you come to the A4 (Bath Road). Here you can turn right and make your way back to the old Town Hall, where you started.

Jubilee River (a little to the east of our route)

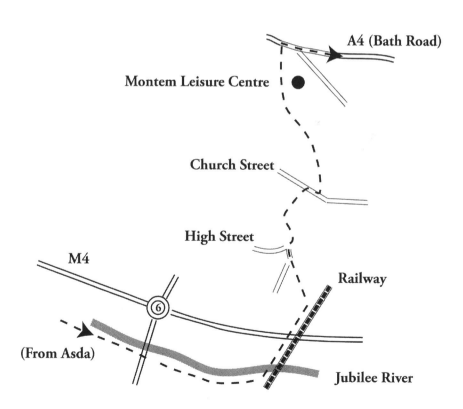

WALK 10

The Outer Circle

This is a complete circuit of the town, at almost marathon length. The distance is about 37km and it takes from six to ten hours to complete. It is the kind of walk that you do when you simply need a challenge.

The route includes parts of some of the other walks described in this book, but adds some new sections. On the whole, it is surprisingly rural.

This chapter consists of an account of my own first attempt at the walk, in the middle of December 2012. As you will gather, it is probably wiser to do it at a drier time of year.

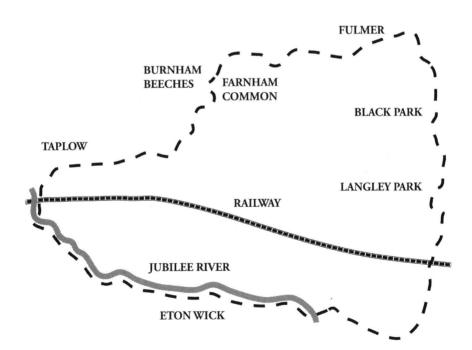

Section 1   Jubilee River from The Myrke to Taplow

Distance: 10.5km

For the last fortnight I've been battling a man-cold and I've reached that end-of-the-tether, guy-thing stage when a decisive physical duel seems the only way forward. So I've challenged it to a trial of strength which only one of us may survive: a full orbit of Slough or death. Yesterday, on the say-so of a woman in Boots, I provisioned with weapons-grade decongestant and I've been backing it up with brufen. *Self polypharmacy*, addiction specialists call this kind of thing.

On the packet the decongestant says "non-drowsy". And that is spot-on — it has kept me awake all night. Not a wink. Finally I leave the house at 07.45 just as dawn is breaking. There's a fox in the garden. I hope it's a good omen.

At 08.15 I reach the Jubilee River at the Myrke. The dry sunny morning promised by the forecasters is a no-show. Instead it's cold and cloudy and there's a raw west wind carrying enough moisture to justify my waterproofs. The river is high and the bridleway is sloppy. It's been a curious year: first we all worried about drought, then about flooding. Just a few days ago I found my route to Datchet blocked at Black Potts where the Jubilee had "overtopped" its bank and the path was under two feet of rushing water.

A useful benchmark for flood defences is that they should not themselves flood — especially when they have cost over £100 million to build. So it's easy to see why people from Wraysbury and Datchet are angry about the Jubilee River, and have been angry since it got the go-ahead in 1995. It might well save Maidenhead and Windsor from flooding, they argued back then, but only by diverting the water on to us. And they were proved right in January 2003, less than a year after its official opening, when the structure failed and hundreds of their houses were inundated. It was a fiasco that eventually cost the designers almost £3 million in an out-of-court settlement.

But, dodgy flood-defender or no, the Jubilee does make a popular park. Even on this squally December morning there are runners, cyclists and dog-walkers on the bridleway and anglers on the bank. And, being navigationally straightforward, it makes a good stage on a challenge walk. Which is to say, I can switch off mentally and ignore the map until I (almost) run out of river.

By 08.50 I'm level with Eton Wick. At 09.10 I go past the Pineapple pub and hear the bells of Dorney church. At 09.50 I reach the A4 near Maidenhead. Hey, that's not bad: 10km in just over 90 minutes. I'd expected two hours. Must be the drugs. On a proper challenge walk I'd cop a doping-ban.

95

Section 2   A4 (Taplow) to Burnham Beeches

Distance: 9km

Today I'm not on puppet safari so there's no need to go through Taplow village. Instead I cross the A4, go along Berry Hill road, and then take a more direct path to Burnham. It starts just 200m up the road, after a recreation ground, and goes obliquely off to the right, through grassy fields. I can see it was once surfaced with tarmac, but most of that has crumbled away. Just south of Taplow village the path joins our puppet route and then follows it eastward over Boundary Road.

At 10.20 I reach Burnham. On the way the sunken path called the New Cut is familiar but still nicely mysterious. Burnham is a ghost town this morning. By the pond a woman is scooping bread from a wheelie-bag for the benefit of a noisy throng of ducks. But there's no-one else around. On the High Street several shops are boarded up. And the chip shop is shut otherwise I'd march hungrily in.

I continue along the puppet route, following the bridleway by the Grammar School. Then I bid the marionettes farewell and join the Robert Cochrane route: across Lynch Hill Park and through Cocksherd Wood. I reach Farnham Lane at 10.50. I've now been walking for three hours. I'm sweating a lot and I swig constantly from my water bottle, but my head has cleared.

Crow Piece Lane is less scruffy and litter-strewn than when I was last here. But beyond the bridleway the footpath seems even more overgrown, even more tightly squeezed between hedge and railing. I'm glad when it crosses the road, even though somebody's been monkeying with the signpost, which now directs me over a barbed-wire fence and through a field full of horses. I ignore it and stay on the broad, dry path which traces three sides of a square around the field before bringing me to a tarmac road.

Now I have to go left for 150m till a footpath goes off to the right. There's a stile, a paddock, another stile, another paddock and then another stile — and then I hit the road that goes round the perimeter of Burnham Beeches. I turn right and go along it for 150m until I reach the Stag pub. I walk through the car park opposite the pub and go out at its left-hand corner, on a path that goes immediately into trees and comes soon to the Middle Pond. Here I turn left on a broad path and follow it for 200m, then leave it to go over a grassy area on my right and come in almost no time to the Druid's Oak, beside a traffic-free road. By the tree is a wooden shelter with a bench that seems to proclaim *Lunchtime*. It's only 11.35 but I've been going for almost four hours.

Eating a sandwich I think about Robert Cochrane. How weird it must have seemed to come up here from Britwell in a car full of robed and cowled witches, the boot filled with cauldrons, stangs and swords and all the other pagan paraphernalia, and then to spend the night chanting and throwing soup around.

And I think about David Icke and his followers, who insist our planet is controlled by aliens that use the Beeches for shape-shifting practice, yet who don't let that belief rouse them to revolt — or indeed let it influence their behaviour at all. Colonised by reptoids? Oh well, mustn't grumble.

I consider asking at the Beeches visitor centre about pagan rituals and reptilian manifestations, but decide against. I'm sweaty and muddy and goggle-eyed from lack of sleep and I fear it might go badly.

Section 3   Burnham Beeches to Fulmer

Distance: 6km

I know the Beeches well, from navigation courses and Nordic walking sessions, and I'm confident on its labyrinth of footpaths. But now, ten-minute lunch-break over, I opt for the luxury of dry tarmac and turn right on the road, knowing it will take me past the visitor centre and cafe and then into Farnham Common. In a village shop I restock with fluid, choosing a calorie-dense sports drink coloured like paint-ball ammunition.

The next section is new ground for me so the OS map comes out, and the compass. The route is well signposted and I soon reach the attractive woods called Ingrams Copse. The efforts of mountain bikers to improve the footpath here have not been successful, however. It's a linear shrine to mud.

At 12.45 I come to the main part of Stoke Common. It's wild and desolate and sort of exhausted and — a surprising thing to feel in South Bucks — it reminds me of the bleaker bits of the Cairngorms and even of a trek I once did in Lapland.

It is *very* wet underfoot: some puddles would justify an aqualung. Near the Fulmer end I meet a woman who, like me, is tip-toeing through the slop. A local resident, she says she is unhappy with the current management of the Common. The authorities want to restore it to the original heathland state but she thinks they've gone too far: by cutting down so many trees, they've affected the drainage and the water table has risen. Certainly, it is an absolute mess today, a quagmire. I leave it ahead of schedule and go out on to the road.

At 13.00 I reach Fulmer. Pretty place, centred, as picture-book English villages should be, around church and pub. I recall the newspaper story about Angelina Jolie and Brad Pitt making the Black Horse their local when they had a house nearby, handy for Pinewood Studios.

"Brad likes a Guinness and Angelina a pint of cider," the landlord told the reporter, expertly seizing the superb marketing opportunity. The pub is haunted, too, he deftly pointed out, and has a ghostly carriage that goes creakily up the lane before vanishing in swirly mist.

I snort at the idea. Even at his most expansive Robert Cochrane would have stopped short of that — an Afterlife for vehicles.

My cynicism is born of fatigue. Driven back from my nasal passages, the man-cold has launched a campaign against my legs. Defensively I break open another bottle of the paint-ball ammo and pop some more brufen.

Section 4   Fulmer to The Myrke

Distance: 7km to canal, then 5km to The Myrke

At 13.55 I reach Black Park Lake, where an oompah band is playing Christmas carols near the cafe. Among the respectable listeners I feel conspicuous, for there is mud up to my knees. The stage from Fulmer has been okay, a country path to begin with then a narrow tarmac road between the imposing houses of Fulmer Common. The *uncommon* ones must be really something. Then there was a few minutes' walk along Black Park Road before I could take a "permissive path" into the park itself.

From the oompah bandstand I follow the Colne Valley Trail, but only for a couple of minutes. Then I take a short cut to the right, due south, soon go across the Uxbridge Road, then go a little to the right before turning down the long driveway to Langley Park House.

At 14.35 I reach the Slough Arm of the Grand Union Canal. The footbridge over it is fine, but the adjoining one, over the railway, is fenced off, closed for rebuilding works, and I have to detour west along the towpath to St Mary's Road, then make my way through St Mary's churchyard and pick up the Green Drive track. Now I'm on very familiar ground, reversing the literature walk, and I put away the map.

At 15.00 I cross the A4 (London Road) and enter Ditton Park, relieved to find the gate still unlocked. The notice says "open till six", but it will soon be dark and I've been worrying that the keepers might close it early.

At 15.30 I reach *The End*, which for me is the M4 footbridge in Upton Court Park. I don't feel I need to cross it again. I've completed the circuit. Job done.

Anyway, I've been walking almost non-stop for nearly seven hours and my legs feel as if strong men have been hitting them with hammers. I've had enough. On the bright side, my man-cold foe lies vanquished — humiliated. And I'm supremely confident I'll have no problem sleeping tonight.

Cheered by these thoughts I turn up through the park and head for home.

REFERENCES AND READING

Anderson, S. (2007) *My FAB Years.* Pennsylvania: Hermes Press.

Archer, S. and Hearn, M. (2002) *What Made Thunderbirds Go! The authorized biography of Gerry Anderson.* London: BBC Worldwide.

Bowerman, D. (1976) *Historic Thames Valley Taverns.* Bourne End, Buckinghamshire: Spurbooks.

Card, T. (1994) *Eton Renewed. A History from 1860 to the present day.* London: John Murray.

Cooper, S. (1973) *The Dark is Rising.* London: Chatto & Windus.

Deloney, T. (1827 edition) *The History of Thomas of Reading.* London : W. Pickering. A digitized facsimile can be downloaded free of charge through the Hathi Trust at *http://hdl.handle.net/2027/uc2.ark:/13960/t1bk1bq2x.*

Fraser, M. (1973) *The History of Slough.* Available free of charge in PDF format from the website of Slough History Online. (*www.sloughhistoryonline. org.uk*; search for Fraser.)

Gray, T. (1751) *Elegy Written in a Country Churchyard.* A free Kindle edition is available through Amazon.

Hollis, C. (1960) *Eton.* London: Hollis & Carter.

Hoskin, M. (2011) *Discoverers of the Universe – William and Caroline Herschel.* Oxford: Princeton University Press.

Hunter, J. and Thompson, I. (1991) *Slough: A Pictorial History.* Chichester: Phillimore Press.

Huxley, A (1932) *Brave New World.* London: Chatto & Windus.

Jones, E. J. and Cochrane, R. (Edited by Howard, M.) (2001) *The Roebuck in the Thicket – an anthology of the Robert Cochrane Witchcraft Tradition.* Milverton (Somerset): Capall Bann Publishing.

Kennish, J. (1999) *Datchet Past.* Chichester: Phillimore Press.

King, J. (2000) *Human Punk.* London: Jonathan Cape.

La Riviere, S. (2009) *Filmed in Supermarionation.* Pennsylvania: Hermes Press.

Long, R. (1990) *Murder in Old Berkshire, a collection of sudden deaths in and around the old county.* Buckingham: Barracuda Books Limited.

Petticrew, I. and Austin, W. *A Highway Laid With Water. An account of the Grand Junction Canal, 1792 - 1928, with a postscript.* This is an online publication, at *http://gerald-massey.org.uk/Canal/index.htm.* Chapter 12 includes details of George Smith.

Poole, W. "Milton's Scholarship 1632-1641" in Jones, E (ed) (2013) *Young Milton, the emerging author 1620-1642.* Oxford. Oxford University Press.

Rowlands, S. (2003) *Around Iver.* Stroud: Tempus Publishing.

Slough Borough Council (2010) *The Index of Multiple Deprivation 2010, SLOUGH.* Available to download from *http://static.slough.gov.uk/downloads/Slough-IMD-Report.pdf.*

Smales, N (2015) *Taplow Moments.* Taplow: published by the author. (Nigel Smales kindly confirmed a location on the puppet walk.)

Tomalin, C. (1990) *The Invisible Woman: The Story of Nelly Ternan and Charles Dickens.* London: Viking.

Tony Ward's site *A Glossary of Canal Boating Terms* is at *https://sites.google.com/site/canalglossary/home.*

BUS TIMES

The following websites give maps and timetables for most local services:

www.firstgroup.com

www.arrivabus.co.uk

TRAIN TIMES

For timetables go to *www.nationalrail.co.uk.*

Printed in Great Britain
by Amazon